Discovering
ENGLAND'S TREES

Miles Hadfield

Shire Publications Ltd

CONTENTS

I must particularly thank Mr. H. L. Edlin of the Forestry Commission for his help and for putting me in touch with that most co-operative and forward-looking body, its Conservators, who supplied me with much local information.

The cover design is by Ron Shaddock.

Copyright © 1970 and 1980 by Miles Hadfield. First published 1970. Second edition 1980. No. 86 in the Discovering series. ISBN 0 85263 490 0.
   All rights reserved. No part of this publication may be reproduced or transmitted in any form or by any means, electronic or mechanical, including photocopy, recording, or any information storage and retrieval system, without permission in writing from the publishers, Shire Publications Ltd, Cromwell House, Church Street, Princes Risborough, Aylesbury, Bucks, HP17 9AJ, UK.
Printed in Great Britain by C. I. Thomas & Sons (Haverfordwest) Ltd, Press Buildings, Merlins Bridge, Haverfordwest.

THE BEGINNING

The natural covering of much of England is woodland. If man disappeared, the trees would reappear and, in all but infertile soils, slowly dominate the landscape.

The story of our forests as they are today begins with the end of the ice age which, it is said, covered the whole of our islands, with perhaps the exceptions of a few small areas. As the ice receded northwards at a time when we were still joined to the continent of Europe, so the vegetation and trees followed it. The kinds are identical with those we know now—not the strange species of the pre-glacial era. Scientists can identify them by means of their pollen grains, each one having its own identifiable structure which remain unaltered in certain types of ground.

The return migration spread over thousands of years until, somewhere around 4000 B.C., our bridge with Europe finally sank beneath the sea, the gap becoming so wide that wind-borne seeds could no longer be carried over it.

The trees growing here immediately after that event are those termed our natives. The very many other kinds that subsequently arrived were all brought by man. They are the introduced or exotic (used in its true sense meaning introduced from abroad) trees.

Our principal native trees, which are those which would eventually form our woods if man left, include the two oaks, the common or pedunculate oak (*Quercus robur*), plate 1, with short-stalked leaves and acorns on long stalks, which would eventually dominate our forests on rich, fertile soils and which would be replaced on somewhat lighter soils in hillier places by the sessile or durmast oak (*Q. petraea*—the word *petraea* meaning 'growing in stony places' accurately hints at its habitat), plate 2. Two kinds of birch grow all over our heaths and on our hills. There is the common silver birch, identified by its twigs being rough from many tiny warts, and without hairs (*Betula verrucosa*), plate 3, which grows in dry situations and another kind (*B. pubescens*) which has smooth, downy shoots and grows in the colder, damper places.

The alder, with fruits like little pine cones, is the tree of really wet situations. In its botanical name *Alnus glutinosa*, *glutinosa* meaning sticky refers to the twigs and buds. Also growing in moist places are the white and crack willows. The former, making a tall, rather rectangular shaped tree, is at once identified by its narrow, almost silver-coloured leaves, and is appropriately named *Salix alba*. The crack willow is a

3

wide-spreading tree whose fine twigs can be snapped off with very little pressure. It is well named *S. fragilis*.

We have two native elms. The wych elm (*Ulmus glabra*), a spreading tree with branches that usually droop at their ends and leaves that are rough to the touch, is found in our woods all over Britain, but more so in the cooler and wetter districts of the north and west. The hedgerow elm (*U. procera*) is a feature of our more fertile areas, almost always found, as its name implies, in connection with agriculture, plate 11. Its origin is unknown—perhaps it arose as a seedling in the Severn Vale—and it is restricted to England. It produces no seed, but increases from suckers which run along the hedgerows. In early times man found that its foliage, which hangs late on the trees, provided useful fodder in the winter. Both elms have strong timber which is durable when kept consistently either wet or dry. It was bored and used for water pipes and much for interior framing of houses: 'old oak' beams are sometimes really elm. The branches were lopped and stored. It owes its distribution entirely to man's activities.

We are now all familiar with the depressing sight of dead elms against the British skyline, but as living trees these once gracious landmarks have almost ceased to exist. Since the arrival of the beetles carrying Dutch elm disease to England in about 1927 (the name Dutch was earned by its first identification in Europe in Holland in 1919) almost no elms have been planted. The deadly disease is a native of North America, and the beetle or its eggs may have been introduced in timber imported through south-western ports and later transported into the west midlands.

Another native which has been widely spread by planting in hedges, particularly during the era of enclosure acts in the eighteenth and early nineteenth centuries, is the hawthorn (*Crataegus monogyna*), plate 6. This is another tree not found in mature woods but playing a part in their formation. When land is neglected, its seedlings arising from the 'haws' eaten by birds who evacuate the hard seeds within, form a scrub into which the seeds of forest trees may well be carried to germinate and grow under the protection of the spiny thorns.

Two other natives, now rarities, but abundant in our forests at that stage when our climate was moister and warmer than it is now, are the large and small-leaved limes (*Tilia platyphyllos* and *T. cordata*); the lime commonly grown particularly in avenues is a hybrid between the two (*T. europaea*) introduced, perhaps in the sixteenth century, from the continent.

Then there is the ash (*Fraxinus excelsior*) distributed widely over our islands, spread by its wind-borne seeds, plate 4.

There are two important natives, however, which originally had a limited natural distribution. One is the beech (*Fagus sylvatica*), probably one of the last trees to arrive before the sea parted us from Europe. It was a tree of the southern counties before man planted it all over our islands. The other is the hornbeam (*Carpinus betulus*), plate 10, with an even more restricted distribution in the south-eastern counties—and not being so valuable commercially as beech, not so frequently found elsewhere.

Other native trees of less importance in our woodlands are

the poplars. The aspen, *Populus tremula,* with its well-known leaves on long flat stalks which cause them to tremble in the slightest wind, is found at the edges and in clearings of woodland. The old native black poplar (*P. nigra betulifolia*) is still occasionally found in open situations. The grey poplar (*P. canescens*) now almost always a planted tree is also believed to be a native. The wild cherry or gean (*Prunus avium*) we can also claim—though many of those found in the edges of woods are seedlings of cultivated trees. The same applies to the wild crab-apples (*Malus sylvestris*).

The well-named field maple (*Acer campestris*) is also scarcely a woodland tree. The rowan or mountain ash (*Sorbus aucuparia*), plate 5, which grows naturally higher up our mountains than any other native, and our other sorbus, the whitebeam (*S. aria*), again are scarcely forest trees.

All these trees, it will be noticed, are deciduous—that is, the leaves unfold in the spring, carry out their duty in helping the tree's life-cycle, and then fall before the winter. They are also called hardwoods—in fact a rather meaningless term, for in some the timber is very soft. The natural forest of the British Isles consists virtually of this kind of tree—it is deciduous forest. The only native evergreen hardwood we shall find scattered in it is the holly (*Ilex aquifolium*) though very dubiously we might include the box (*Buxus sempervirens*). (In an evergreen the life-cycle of a leaf is not completed for, perhaps, three or four years on the tree, when it falls).

Yet vast areas of the world's forests consist naturally of mostly evergreen* coniferous trees or softwoods, and are of an entirely different nature to Britain's native forests. The structure of the timber, the leaves and the fertilization and production of seeds (in cones) is quite different from that in our hardwoods. (Here again, the term softwoods, so widely used, is not really apt as some have extremely hard timber).

Our native woodland conifers are of two kinds only, the Scots pine and the yew, the juniper being a shrub rather than a tree. The Scots pine (*Pinus sylvestris*) as a native tree is restricted to Scotland, having been so to speak driven into retreat there owing to changes in the climate. The yew (*Taxus baccata*) is found as a self-sown native scattered in many woodlands and very occasionally as the principal constituent of small woods found mostly in the south on chalk downs. The scales of the cone in this tree instead of being tough and leathery are merged together to form the soft berry-like container of the seed.

---

* Not all conifers are evergreen—a notable exception is the larch—but most are.

Those, then, were the principal trees which covered most of the country when we became an island. Their actual proportions in the woodland varied from time to time in accordance with climatic changes (which are still occurring today). For instance, during the period of the Sub-boreal climate, the lime was a prominent forest tree, instead of the rarity that it later became. Somewhere around 700 B.C. the climate became wetter and cooler, much peat was formed and destroyed areas of birch-pine forest whose remains, preserved in the peat, are sometimes unearthed today—the 'buried forests', which also occur when land has been flooded by the sea. The proportion of hazel (*Corylus avellana*), an important constituent of woodland but scarcely a tree, also varied. It is generally believed that the last arrival to establish itself here was beech.

Since man's arrival, and particularly during the last four centuries, he has destroyed most of the natural forest—first to provide an agricultural economy and second to provide an industrial one. In the present century circumstances have forced him to replace some of what he has ravaged. And this he has done largely by planting conifers—for reasons which will be explained later—instead of hardwoods.

TREES AND THE ENGLISHMAN

The first man to arrive here can have had little effect on the dense woodland. With neolithic man came agriculture—and the fertile land was covered with dense oak forest. It was probably cleared by burning, the resulting ash adding fertility to the land. By the end of this period the goat and the sheep had been introduced. As is well known, deserts have been created when goats become dominant. When sheep get into woods, they destroy the seedling trees, natural reproduction ceases, old trees decay and at last the woods become lifeless.

In due course Iron Age man arrived and with him came another need (and eventually a very destructive one) for timber from our forests: timber to provide fuel for smelting. Even so, the effect on our vast areas of woodland was insignificant. It is probable that Iron Age man was the first to introduce trees from the Continent—maybe better kinds of fruit—apples and pears—than we possessed and perhaps elms used for winter fodder. This is now held by some to be the case with the smooth-leaved elm (*Ulmus carpinifolia*) found, along with its hybrids with the two natives, in East Anglia.

If that was so, then from that time onwards the introduction of trees from overseas has been regularly practiced, for food, ornament and timber production. Certainly the Romans brought trees with them, though there is some doubt which. They are credited with the sweet chestnut (*Castanea sativa*), plate 13, presumably for its nuts (we had an abundance of equally good or better timber). Probably they also brought the walnut (*Juglans regia*) quite certainly for its nuts, not probably entirely for eating but because they were the only source of a valuable vegetable oil that would thrive in England; we cannot, for instance, grow the olive.

There can be little doubt that other trees were introduced during the 'dark ages' that followed, but which kinds seem uncertain. Timber being so abundant, they were probably fruit—better apples, pears or plums.

The importance of our woodlands, clearings in them, and individual trees as landmarks at this time and later is well shown by the many place names still including such elements as *oak*—and *ac*—(oak), *al*—(alder), *mapul*—(maple), *ash*—and *aesc*—(ash), *aps*—and *esp*—(aspen). All are English natives. Sometimes, these are still applicable but often, principally owing to urbanization, their significance is lost. Terms indicating clearings in woodland, such as *ley*, are also common. The Saxon charters delineating boundaries often name trees by their kinds as landmarks, which gives us an idea of those species commonly found in a given area. Incidentally, Saxon buildings were preponderantly of timber, not stone.

The Domesday survey is in many ways a disappointment for the tree historians. It was more or less a valuation of land and a register of who owned it. Unlike in the Saxon charters, therefore, no individual tree (despite a general belief to the contrary!) is mentioned. It consequently describes woodland in rather vague terms of area, but frequently with regard to what we should now call their 'productivity'—the number of pigs that could be turned out into them to fatten on the mast (the ripe acorns and beech nuts).

In Norman times the royal forests and the brutal laws concerning them were codified. They were concerned with hunting, being areas outside the common law*. Their first aim was the preservation of deer for sport; for this purpose much of the land was open and not densely wooded. The modern use of the word 'forest' as a place where trees are grown is, therefore, quite different from the original meaning—though some of the old royal forest areas, often now thickly planted as they provide good conditions for growing trees, have become our modern forests: New and Dean are examples.

---

* The last king to enforce this forest law was Charles I; they were repealed in 1640.

The assault on our woodlands gained considerable force under the Normans, curiously owing to the introduction and development of their religious houses. These were mostly of an urban nature. The Cistercians on the other hand were farmers. In 1132 after settling at Rievaulx in Yorkshire the order rapidly developed its activities, usually in remote and wooded areas. Much ground was cleared for corn, but the most significant damage was done by their large scale sheep-farming; at one time Melrose Abbey had some 12,000 breeding sheep, which entered the woods razing all young trees. The effect on natural reproduction (called by foresters regeneration) was catastrophic.

Meanwhile, in spite of set backs such as the Black Death, our economy was developing fast. By the time the Tudors came into power, we were building more houses, more ships (and the harbours for them), smelting more iron, drying more brine to produce salt, using more oak bark for tanning leather and making glass; brewers needed more oak for their casks. Coal was slowly coming into use for producing heat but no more; until the mid eighteenth century it could not produce an equivalent for the charcoal essential for our ironmasters.

Woodland and timber, instead of being over-abundant, was becoming of increased value. Among the biggest owners of it were the monasteries (not only the Cistercians). In 1536 they were suppressed. Some prescient abbots and priors had, before that, been felling and turning their best timber into cash—a much more movable asset. After the dissolution, the monastic woods were disposed of by agents of the Crown (corruption was general) to the new aristocracy who felled recklessly and with no considered policy to save good young trees for the future, to finance their purchases.

During the latter part of the reign of Henry VIII and of the reign of Edward VI the first attempts by law were made to halt this wastage of what had once been so abundant. In 1580 the great Burleigh ordered a sowing of acorns in Windsor Park. This is believed to be the first occasion on which the Englishman, not nature, tried to restore his ravaged woods; today it is the usual practice.

The key to the situation was oak, particularly the so-called English oak, *Q. robur*. With its rugged much-angled branching, and immensely strong timber, plate 1, it was the skeleton of the ships, not only for Elizabeth I's navy, but for her steadily increasing fleet of merchantmen, as well as for the framing of buildings. The sessile oak (*Q. petraea*), plate 2, with its straighter growth was not nearly so useful.

The history of our oakwoods at this time and for long after

was the perpetual and generally losing struggle of the navy to acquire the massive, inevitably old trees for its ships in face of competition—often the State itself—from the more remunerative sale of younger trees for the many other purposes for which timber was demanded.

Here it may be remarked that from this time until today (when it is even more the case) the financial, profit-making aspect of timber growing has been of the greatest importance. A tree that can be sold profitably at a younger age than one that occupies the ground much longer to bring in an only slightly increased return on the capital involved is the better investment.

The shortage of ships timber at the time of the Restoration was acute, putting the navy in danger, official policy during the Commonwealth having been aimed at these quick financial returns, without any planning of future planting. In 1662 the 'Honourable Principal Officer, and Commissioners of the Navy' put to the newly formed Royal Society a paper of inquiries into the dire situation. On 15th October of that year John Evelyn recorded "I this day delivered my Discourse concerning Forest-trees to our Society upon the occasion of Certaine Queries sent us by the Commissioners of His Majesties Navy." This was considered of such great importance by the Fellows that it was issued, greatly elaborated, as the Society's first publication in 1664. Known as *Sylva*, it was a study of the trees we then grew, showing Evelyn's amazing knowledge. It was and is of great importance, including as it does the first full accounts of trees that had been introduced from overseas partly for their possible economic use as well as to satisfy the band of 'curious gardeners' and botanists that had arisen during and since Elizabethan days. As some are now of consequence in our plantations, it is interesting to describe them in their order of arrival.

First came the sycamore (*Acer pseudoplatanus*), a native of the mountains of central southern Europe, which was being grown in Scotland probably during the fifteenth and certainly during the sixteenth century. Helped by man, it soon spread south and is now naturalised in most parts of the British Isles. In Scotland it is still often called a plane. There is reason in this, as the shape of the leaves resembles those of that tree: they are however carried on the twigs opposite to one another instead of alternately as on the plane. The fruit, too, consists of 'keys', while those of the plane are in balls. Why it is called the sycamore is unknown: it has no resemblance in any way to the true sycamore, which is a fig, *Ficus sycomorus*. The white, clean wood was long valued for such things as dairy utensils—today, especially if 'figured' with a pattern, it is valued for ornamental purposes. Unfortunately, it is often damaged by the grey squirrel in search of the watery sap. It is immensely hardy and firmly rooted; old trees are often seen protecting farmsteads in exposed, mountainous situations (plate 12).

Probably the next arrival was the Norway spruce (*Picea abies*) from northern Europe, now one of our commonest forest trees. It is grown to supply Christmas trees and valuable timber. An early record of its presence is in 1548 when it was grown as an ornament.

Another arrival at about this time was the oriental plane (*Platanus orientalis*), plate 16, brought, presumably, because of the high esteem in which it was regarded by the ancients; its beauty caused Xerxes to halt his prodigious army to admire it. It is this tree too, that is so often seen in Persian art. Though still not common, it is one parent of the ubiquitous London plane (*Platanus hybrida*), plate 15.

Probably the silver fir (*Abies alba*) a native of central and southern Europe was also brought here about this time. A valuable timber tree in its native land, and not uncommon with us, it suffers so badly from attacks of a gall-forming aphid, fungus infections and late frosts that it is now rarely grown in our forests.

It might be appropriate here to refer to one main difference between the outwardly rather similar spruces (*Picea*) and firs (*Abies*). The spruce has cones that are always more or less pendulous, shedding their seeds by dropping them when the scales part, the cones themselves usually falling entire and lying for some time under the tree. The cones of the firs are erect and shed their seeds by disintegrating on the tree, leaving only their central spike-like axis behind.

In Evelyn's day the evergreen holm oak or ilex (*Quercus ilex*) was still not common; he suggests that it was introduced from the Mediterranean about 1580. This, too, is a handsome tree with classical illusions and one that will stand our windy, seaside conditions. Though without economic value it was often planted, becoming very fashionable in the early eighteenth century.

In 1597 we have the first record of a tree brought from eastern North America, an area that was later (together with the west) to be the source of many trees that we grow. The conifer, arbor-vitae, (*Thuya occidentalis*) was in Evelyn's time being planted for ornament. It has no value as a timber tree and many much more attractive conifers have taken its place in gardens.

In 1629 the larch, (*Larix europaea*) now one of our commonest timber producing conifers and one of the few that drops its leaves in winter, was not common "in our land, and nursed up but with a few, and those only lovers of rarities . . . the blossoms are very beautiful and delectable, being of an excellent fine crimson colour, which standing among the green leaves, allure the eyes of the beholders to regard it with the more desire."

Shortly afterwards the false acacia or locust tree (*Robinia pseudacacia*), having a very limited distribution in North America, arrived here via the Jardin des Plantes in Paris, where it was first grown by Vespasien Robin—hence the name. Spreading by means of suckers, it is now locally common and in its various forms still often planted. At one time, following enthusiastic claims made for it by William Cobbett, it was planted for timber production. The wood unfortunately soon proved to be useless because it splits very easily,

By 1633 John Tradescant had a good specimen of the horse-chestnut growing in his garden at Lambeth. This also presumably arrived here via Paris where in 1615 a certain M. Bachelier had received seed from Constantinople. As it was grown by the Turks, then a nation famed as gardeners, for its beauty as well as the value of its nuts in curing coughing horses* it was long believed to be a native of Turkey. Less than a century ago this was found to be wrong: it is a relic of an ancient era of plant life restricted to remote parts of Albania and Greece. Evelyn wished, though, that "we did more propagate" a tree that was "now all the mode for the avenues to their country palaces in France" with "a most glorious flower, even in our cold country."

Evelyn discussed every aspect of the trees known to him from the legends that surrounded them in antiquity to their uses and propagation. He referred to many fine specimens, but probably only one, the great chestnut by the church at Tortworth in Avon, still survives.

By the time Evelyn wrote, the Scots pine brought down from its retreat in Scotland was becoming naturalised on the heathland in Surrey, and the white poplar (*P. alba*) from Europe was also finding itself at home here. He also mentions that the hybrid lime, already mentioned, (*Tilia europaea*) was being imported in large numbers from Holland to form the great avenues so admired in the days of the Stuarts.

Another famous tree mentioned by Evelyn is the cedar of Lebanon, plate 24; of this, he wrote that he "received cones

---

* 'horse' is not, as often stated, used here in the sense of coarse, e.g. horse-radish.

and seeds of those few remaining trees".* From this it has been assumed that he introduced the tree which, however, is known to have been planted at Wilton House in Wiltshire by 1640. The name cedar, from the Greek *kedros,* an unidentifiable tree with fragrant wood, has been applied in the vernacular to many trees with those qualities which do not belong to the botanist's genus *Cedrus,* or even to conifers.

He was rather confused over the pines, two of which—still uncommon trees—were growing here in his time. *Pinus pinea* the stone pine, plate 21, the 'open umbrella' tree of the Italian landscape of Claude and similar painters, whose imported cones and edible seeds, pignons, played a part in the religion of our Roman invaders, is believed to have been growing here by 1548. The pinaster, *P. pinaster,* from the coastal regions of the Mediterranean, was probably here in 1596. With us, it is only locally common near the sea, as at Bournemouth.

Evelyn does not mention the deciduous swamp cypress (*Taxodium distichum*), plate 26. This native of the southeastern parts of North America, a beautiful, stately tree with light green, feathery foliage turning gold before the leaves fall, has been a distinguished ornament of our gardens and parks since 1640. He does, however, mention another eastern American tree: "they have a poplar of Virginia of a very peculiar shaped leaf as if the point of it were cut off, which grows very well with the curious amongst us to a considerable stature. I conceive it was first brought over by John Tradescant, under the name of the tulip-tree (from the likeness of its flower) . . . I wish we had more of them". *Liriodendron tulipifera,* one of the most handsome deciduous trees we can grow, was no doubt introduced, probably about 1658, because of its valuable timber, but it has never become a forest tree here. The golden-yellow of its fiddle-shaped leaves in autumn is unsurpassed.

AFTER EVELYN

The first edition of *Sylva* was sold within two years. In the second, the dedication to Charles II claimed that the work had been "the sole occasion of furnishing your almost exhausted Dominions with more than two millions of timber trees." That is probably an overstatement, as oak for ships timber remained in short, generally dangerously short, supply,

---

* The trees on Mount Lebanon were being pillaged for their timber even in the days when Solomon's temple was being built.

for the rest of this period and almost until its use for that purpose ceased.

Evelyn's enthusiasm had, however, stimulated the English to plant and experiment with trees, especially new kinds introduced from abroad.

Earlier, such men as Edward Seymour, Duke of Somerset, who died in 1552, had planted many new kinds in the magnificent garden he made at Syon House. The John Tradescants, father and son, were important collectors and cultivators of novelties: the father's catalogue of trees that he grew at Lambeth in 1634 is an important historical document; his son's comparable list of 1656 shows a further increase in trees from most of the temperate parts of the world. Another famous pioneer of tree planting, Henry Compton, while Bishop of London from 1657 to 1713, grew a great variety of trees, many of them new-comers, at Fulham Palace. (His successor, more interested in vegetables, disposed of most of them.)

There were now many other landowners who were ardent arboriculturists experimenting with trees either because of the new scientific curiosity that followed the formation of the Royal Society or in the hope of finding kinds that would produce better timber than our natives. From this and ancient woodland history it became clear that Britain's climate enabled an enormous variety of foreign trees to be grown.

Evelyn may or may not have seen the now famous London plane, (*Platanus hybrida* or *acerifolia*). It is believed to be a hybrid between the oriental plane, already mentioned, and the North American button-wood, *P. occidentalis*. This last does not thrive in this country. The suggestion that the cross occurred in the Oxford Botanic Garden seems untenable, though it seems to have been growing there in about 1666. The vogue for planting it so extensively in London only goes back to the beginning of the last century.

The black walnut, *Juglans nigra,* another eastern North American, provides one of the most valuable of fine quality timbers. With much longer leaves carrying more numerous, sharply-pointed leaflets than the European *Juglans regia,* and with round, inedible nuts, it came here in 1686. There are very many fine specimens, but it has never made the grade here as a timber tree.

The Norway maple (*Acer platanoides*), differentiated from the sycamore by the long-pointed lobes on the leaves and 'keys' paired in a straight line, is first recorded growing in the Edinburgh Botanic Garden in 1683. It has since naturalised itself all over Britain, often entering into woodlands. The timber is not highly valued, but it is a splendid town tree. It naturally has a very wide geographical range—but is not seen at its best in Norway! It has 'sported' some fine crimson-leaved forms.

The Swedish whitebeam (*Sorbus intermedia*) has two apt names—first, it is Scandinavian and secondly the leaves are intermediate between our native service-tree and rowan. It has been much planted for ornament and has been widely distributed by birds who eat the berries; it is not impossible that those flying south from Scandinavia in autumn have brought the tree here, too, though it was introduced by man in 1690.

The end of the century saw the introduction of a pine that was of great importance to us. *Pinus strobus* is called in its native eastern North America the eastern white pine and in this country the Weymouth pine, from the Lord Weymouth who planted it widely at Longleat from about 1705. Its importance was that from it the strongest, tallest masts could be made for our ships (we have no native tree really suitable for this purpose—our mast timber was imported either from North America or from the Baltic). Unlike the pines we have mentioned so far, it has not two but five needles in each leaf bundle. Unfortunately, like many of the trees growing inland in eastern North America, it does not altogether like our insular climate. And like all five-leaved pines it is attacked by a destructive fungus whose alternate hosts are black-currants and gooseberries. It is a beautiful tree, though now rarely planted except for ornament, as it seldom thrives with us. We had to continue importing most of our masts.

Evelyn revised and added to an edition of *Sylva* published in 1706, the year he died. By that time, our timber supply was as precarious as ever. Parliament had passed legislation to preserve and improve the Forest of Dean and the New Forest, two of the now limited number of royal forests remaining today which were then largely given over to growing trees, particularly ships oak, but the new laws were not strictly enforced. All kinds of timber were consumed in the iron furnaces, whose production grew rapidly and spread into new areas (the rate of this destruction had been greatly accelerated by the introduction of the blast furnace in Elizabeth I's reign).

One introduction is particularly concerned with London. In 1726 Mark Catesby, an Englishman who was a remarkable student of the natural history of the eastern states of North America, particularly Carolina, brought back with him on his return the seeds of the Indian bean tree, (*Catalpa bignonioides*) which bears its handsome spikes of flowers and runner-bean-like pods not only in the parks but even in Piccadilly.

The weeping willow (*Salix babylonica*)—which is not the tree under which the Israelites sat and wept, but believed to be a native of China—was brought to England by a Mr. Vernon, a Turkey merchant at Aleppo, from the river Euphrates, in about 1730. Its pendant growth soon became immensely popular sculpted on tombstones and memorials. Today, it is a rare tree, not having been really hardy and having been gradually replaced by a form or hybrid of our native white willow called *Salix alba tristis*.

The Turkey oak came from the Balkans five years later—recognised by the long scales around the buds; though quicker growing than our native oaks it transpired that the timber is much inferior. By 1743 the Chinese opposite number, so to speak, of the American arbor-vitae already mentioned, *Thuya orientalis,* a favourite of Victorian cemeteries, was here. Then from Pekin the missionary Père d'Incarville (even in those days greatly restricted in his movements and activities) sent the handsome tree-of-heaven *Ailanthus altissima,* plate 19—another favourite in the London parks and gardens.

A poplar, the fragrant-leaved 'balm of gilead' *P. candicans* or *gileadensis,* a suckering, usually diseased tree that seems to be happiest scenting spoil-banks,came from an unknown source about 1750. As a contrast, in 1758 there was growing in the nursery of James Gordon at Mile End a specimen of the only surviving member of the *Ginkgoaceae* which in Jurassic times grew in most parts of the world. This, the maidenhair tree (*Ginkgo biloba*), came from Japan. The claim that it had been saved from extinction by Buddhists who for centuries grew it round their temples is now held to be unfounded: trees can still be found growing wild in remote parts of western China.

In the same year, or possibly earlier, came that landmark, the spiring Lombardy poplar (*P. italica*), plate 18; the doubtfully original, but certainly very early specimens still grow at St. Osyth's Priory, Essex, brought there from Turin by the Earl of Rochford when he was our ambassador to Italy.

1759 saw the introduction of what was to become an important timber tree. The Corsican pine (*P. nigra* var. *maritima*) is tall, straight-growing and sombre, somewhat resembling our native Scots pine but without the latter's red glow in the upper part of its trunk. This grows well on poor, light soil.

About 1770 the Italian black poplar, *P. serotina,* another of those hybrids between an American and a European species whose place of origin is not known, was growing here. This tall, sparsely-branched quick-growing tree, leaning permanently away from the prevailing wind, one of the last trees to come into leaf (when it showers down its crimson catkins) is of considerable importance. It was the first of the hybrid poplars of which there are now many kinds whose quick growth makes them a valuable tree for the production of matches and chip-baskets.

The eighteenth century saw a great change, beginning in our landscape and woods. In our gardens and parks the classical formality of France, with balanced, geometric designs based on those developed in France by the great Le Nôtre (1613-1700) with close-clipped hedges and trees in regular avenues, often carried out by the firm of London and Wise with their huge nursery at Brompton in Kensington, was replaced by the informal, landscape garden. This English invention, introduced by writers like Addison and Pope and first executed by designers such as William Kent (whose work is still to be seen at Rousham in Oxfordshire) and landowners such as the Hon. Charles Hamilton at Painshill in Surrey, and Henry Hoare at Stourhead in Wiltshire, entirely changed the nature of gardening. Great numbers of trees planted irregularly in belts and clumps, and the making of natural-looking lakes instead of formal canals, inspired by the paintings of Poussin, Claude, Salvator and others of that period, altered great areas of the English parkland scene, particularly when Lancelot ('Capability') Brown (1716-1783), Humphry Repton (1752-1818) or their followers were employed on a wide scale to 'improve' the old-fashioned gardens. Blenheim Park is a splendid example of what was in its day a revolutionary form of garden design, carried out by Brown.

In our naturally hard-wood English forests, in addition to the Scots pine, another conifer, Norway spruce, was being introduced as a valuable, quick-growing timber tree. An even more sensational change was initiated about 1750 when the then Duke of Atholl began planting larch up in the hills at Dunkeld, eventually in great numbers. The trees thrived, providing valuable timber quickly. The practice soon spread to England, and now there are few woodlands where it is not present, though it remains pre-eminently a Scottish tree.

Yet in spite of the endeavours of enlightened woodland owners, the short supply of suitable naval timber towards the end of the eighteenth century at last frightened the government into activity. The largest owner of good timber producing land, and the one best able to plan on a long term the production of what was needed, was the Crown, still owning considerable tracts of the old royal forests. The management had, for centuries, been largely without plan, and sometimes corrupt. Commissioners under the able chairmanship of

Admiral Sir Charles Middleton were appointed to inquire into the past, present state and future of the royal forests. The reports from 1787 to 1793 were of outstanding value. Their plans for extensive planting and production of ships timber—tough, angular, widespreading oak—were implemented by planting schemes unfortunately not begun until the next century. The first of the mass of new oaks were thus ready for the ship-builders in the present century, long after wooden battleships were obsolete. The trees were practically valueless; what was by then needed was straight oak, such as is suitable for modern structural requirements—the kind produced by the once despised sessile tree. And other timbers of suitable quality for our growing requirements could by now be imported cheaply from many parts of the world. Most of our once fine, picturesque woodland became, as the nineteenth century moved on, a liability rather than asset. Much of it was saved solely for the value of the sport that it provided, particularly for the new rich class of industrialists.

Another significant event, as has been mentioned, was taking place: its consequences to our forests and even scenery were for long not apprehended. Between 1790 and 1795 Captain Vancouver made his famous voyage which included his historic survey up the Pacific coast of North America, until then very little visited. His surgeon-botanist, Archibald Menzies (who on the way there had collected seeds of the Chilean monkey-puzzle (*Araucaria araucana*), plate 22—incidentally not those he was given as dessert—which he introduced to England) discovered or rediscovered, bringing back descriptions, but not living plants of such trees as the Douglas fir, (*Pseudotsuga menziesii*—named in his honour), Sitka spruce (*Picea sitchensis*), Nootka cypress (*Chamaecyparis nootkatensis*) and giant redwood (*Sequoia sempervirens*). It is an interesting and important fact that these American trees from west of the Rockies thrive much better with us—and in many other countries—than do those from the east, which had long been grown here but had not proved to be good timber producers.

THE NINETEENTH CENTURY

The great industrial development of this century was based on coal, iron and steel. Our timber was no longer used in the iron industry, for by about 1775 coke made from coal had replaced wood charcoal. By 1866 import duties had been removed from all commonwealth and foreign timber, which was now cheap.

The nineteenth century was therefore one during which timber growing was not a prosperous business—its products were largely devoted to local building, farm maintenance, wagon making and so on. But it was also a time of great experiment following the introduction of new trees—nearly all done by the owners of private estates. World-wide collections of trees were developed or initiated. Here the new kinds were tested and those that promised yields of timber were propagated and planted in woodlands by a small band of enthusiastic foresters, mostly to become members of what are now the Royal Scottish Forestry Society founded in 1854 and the Royal Forestry Society of England, Wales and Northern Ireland, founded at Hexham, Northumberland, in 1882.

The first well known tree to be introduced in the nineteenth century was not, however, one that had any useful purpose. It was the ornamental red-flowered horse-chestnut (*Aesculus carnea*) which is grown in streets, parks and gardens all over the country. It is another of those remarkable hybrids between trees coming from the New and Old Worlds—in this case between the common horse chestnut and the North American red-flowered buckeye (*Aesculus pavia*). It was apparently first planted here in about 1818.

After that, the most significant date in the history of our trees and woods was undoubtedly 26th July 1824. On it a young Scot, David Douglas, sailed from Gravesend to the north Pacific coast of America. He was despatched by what is now the Royal Horticultural Society to collect seeds of the trees and plants which Archibald Menzies had described during his voyage with Vancouver and which had also been examined by a few travellers visiting what was then a dangerous and little known country.

Douglas, among many other plants and trees now well known in our islands, sent or brought us the first seeds of the giant fir (*Abies grandis*) in 1825, the Douglas fir (*Pseudotsuga menziesii*) in 1827, the 'nobilis' fir (*Abies procera*) in 1830, and the Sitka spruce (*Picea sitchensis*) in 1831. First grown for ornament, within 30 or 40 years their value as producers of valuable crops of timber within half the time taken by any of our native trees had been realised; further, they would do so on land of inferior quality. Today, Sitka spruce is the most extensively planted tree in the British Isles. Douglas was accidentally killed in 1834.

The 'grandis' fir, as it is commonly known, also grows with great speed. The dark green, glossy leaves are rather large for a fir (up to 1½ ins. long or even more) and are in one flat plane on the shoot, not spreading around it.

The Douglas fir is one of the most handsome and largest of conifers, a stately tree with rough bark, pointed buds like a beech, and bracts between the cone scales like Neptune's trident projecting between the cone scales. The timber is first-rate.

'Nobilis' fir* stands out in the forest by the bluish-grey colour of the leaves densely set on and curving upwards around the shoots, and the very large cones five or six inches long so heavy that they often twist over the shoots that carry them.

The Sitka spruce is a dark, sombre tree with short danger-ously prickly leaves projecting all round the twigs. In every way it is the least attractive of the commercial forester's trees, but in certain situations is the best timber producer.

In 1835 Peter Lawson, an Edinburgh nurseryman, first raised seedlings of the Austrian or black pine (*Pinus nigra*). A native of central Europe, it will grow under the worst circumstances. Very similar to the Corsican pine but with an ungainly system of branching and sombre colouring, it is a valuable shelter tree in exposed weather-beaten situations.

1838 saw the arrival of seeds of the Monterey cypress (*Cupressus macrocarpa*), which grows well as a decorative tree in our milder counties, and is also used for hedges. Aylmer Bourke Lambert, one of the greatest authorities on conifers of the day, obtained them from no one knows where and presented some to the Horticultural Society's Chiswick garden. It grows as a native only in a very small, wind-swept district of Monterey Bay in South California along with the Monterey pine (*Pinus radiata*). This is also grown in our milder places, where it will stand the strongest sea gales (to which it is used at home); in some parts of the world it is now a valuable quick-growing timber tree. This, along with the Californian redwood (*Sequoia sempervirens*), the tallest tree in the world and one that we increasingly grow for timber as well as for its beauty—particularly the lovely red trunk—was introduced in 1843 in the most surprising manner. At one time the Russians had a settlement in California, which they abandoned, but not before they had sent home seeds (or perhaps living examples) of many of the plants that they found. In turn, they sent some to us from St. Petersburg Botanic Garden as it then was.

About the same time, the most beautiful weeping silver lime

---

* It was formerly called *A. nobilis;* the name has stuck although under the botanist's rules it was changed to *A. procera.*

(*Tilia petiolaris*) now often seen as a specimen tree, is known to have been growing here. It is a hybrid; where it originated or whence it came no one knows for certain.

Many trees, shrubs and plants had over the centuries arrived here from China and Japan by devious routes. The first British collector to visit China, and later Japan, was another Scot, Robert Fortune. The Horticultural Society first sent him there in 1843. He collected very many trees, shrubs and plants that are now well known in our gardens. Among trees, his large-scale introduction of the Japanese cedar (*Cryptomeria japonica*) in 1844, a widely planted ornamental tree, was the most outstanding.

A year or so later Lord Somers brought seeds of the Atlas cedar (*Cedrus atlantica*), plate 23, from Morocco. Particularly in its grey-blue leaved form, this is now the commonest cedar in England, much more so than the old Lebanon, for the reason that it is a hardier tree, stands town conditions well, and is much more prolific with its seeds.

The interest in conifers was now at its height. In 1849 a body was formed in Edinburgh called the Oregon Association for the purpose of further searching in north-west America. They engaged a young man, John Jeffrey, as collector. At first he sent home good supplies of seed but by 1853 had mysteriously disappeared; no trace was ever found of him. Before this in 1851 he had introduced one of the beautiful and at the same time economically valuable western hemlock (*Tsuga heterophylla*); why it was ever called hemlock remains an unsolved problem. It is a broadly pyramidal tree, the leading shoot lax and whip-like, the slender twigs densely covered with the small, narrow leaves and small cones. It is increasingly grown both for its timber and beauty. Jeffrey also introduced that tall, narrow and statuesque ornamental, the incense cedar (*Calocedrus,* formerly *Libocedrus decurrens*).

By now the enterprising Exeter nurserymen, Veitch's, had realised that there was great enthusiasm for exotic plants. They began to operate on more systematic lines, and on a much larger scale than their predecessors, employing a number of collectors. So far as trees were concerned William Lobb (1809-63) was by far the most important. He was sent not only to collect new kinds, but to collect in large quantities what his predecessors had brought back in small numbers. Thus he re-introduced the monkey puzzle which had remained an expensive rarity, bringing back so many seeds that in 1843 Veitch had thousands for sale. In 1853 he had another spectacular success with the Californian big-tree or wellingtonia (*Sequoiadendron giganteum*), plate 20—the biggest but not the tallest tree in the world. At the same time he brought the beautiful and commercially valuable so-called western red 'cedar' (which it is not) *Thuya plicata*. It is a tall, narrow-crowned tree with dense, fern-like sprays of light green foliage. When crushed this has a distinctive resinous fragrance. There are usually very many small cones. The timber, though not structurally strong, is very resistant to decay, and is widely used for roofing shingles and small wooden buildings. This thuya stands clipping well and is excellent for hedges and screens. It is in almost every way a contrast to its eastern American relative, *Thuya occidentalis* which as we have seen was the first North American tree to be introduced.

Another introduction in 1853 was the Nootka cypress. Menzies had discovered this growing on the shores of Nootka Sound in 1793 though it came to England via a German firm of nurserymen. Botanically, it is not a true cypress (*Cupressus*) but a 'false' cypress, *Chamaecyparis nootkatensis*. The most obvious distinction between the 'true' and the 'false' is that the cross-section of the shoots of foliage in the former is rounded, in the latter flattened and tape-like. The most popular of garden conifers, Lawson's 'cypress' (*Chamaecyparis lawsoniana*) was introduced in 1854 by William Murray who combined a journey to collect Californian trees for the firm of Lawson (which raised the first seedlings) with a search for the missing John Jeffrey. This tree grows naturally only in a restricted area on the Pacific coast of the U.S.A. in a damp and cloudy climate free from frost and excessive heat. Yet there are few places in the British Isles where it will not grow well. Further, under cultivation seedlings began to vary greatly. Erect, tight-growing forms, pendulous forms, blue-grey-leaved forms, yellow-leaved and variegated-leaved forms are all found in gardens and parks. It is distinguished by its fine, fern-like sprays of leaves which when crushed smell like parsley (branches of it are sold by florists) and the small cones about $\frac{3}{8}$ in. diameter, globular until they open. It is only grown to a limited extent in our forests as a timber tree.

Other trees from the west of North America are now grown here principally for ornament as it was soon found that they were not good timber trees. One, the lodge-pole pine (*Pinus contorta*), though introduced by Jeffrey, remained unused in forestry until about 1930 when it was discovered to grow well on very poor, sandy soils.

Many trees and plants from Japan (including a number of kinds that were truly natives only of China but had early been taken into cultivation by the Japanese) made their way here by devious routes. Owing to the Japanese horror of foreigners, and their refusal to let them travel, little collecting was done in the islands. By 1861 the restrictions had been lifted. In that year John Gould Veitch, a member of the firm of nurserymen, went there. He was the first to secure many trophies. The most important was undoubtedly the Japanese larch (*Larix leptolepis*) which grows much more quickly than the European larch and is extensively planted in our forests. It is identified by its red twigs in winter (in the European they are yellowish or grey) and by the upper edge of the cone scales being rolled over outwards (in the European they are erect). The two have hybridised and, under the name of Dunkeld larch (after the place where the cross first occurred), botanically *Larix eurolepis*, the progeny is also grown for its timber.

Veitch also brought two more *Chamaecyparis* species, the Hinoki (*Ch. obtusa*) and the Sawara cypress (*Ch. pisifera*) which were often planted in gardens and churchyards in Victorian days.

We have so far dealt with the now widely grown trees as they came from differing areas as these were explored botanically during the nineteenth century. The majority, and certainly the most important, came from the activities of a mere handful of men: Douglas, Fortune, Jeffrey, Lobb and Veitch.

Other trees which were introduced turned out to be principally ornamental. Many came from the Himalayas like the magnolias. One exception is the noble deodar cedar, the name meaning "the tree of a god" (*Cedrus deodara*). As lax and graceful in form as the other cedars are rigid, this was first introduced in 1831 but was not common until ten years later. The timber is valuable but is little grown in our forests perhaps because it bears little seed in this country and is not easy to propagate; also it is slow growing.

Then there are the Japanese cherries which flower profusely in every suburban street and garden. These are hybrids and forms raised by those masters of horticultural artifice, the Japanese. The first of these was brought over in the early years of the last century, but there were very few until 1892 when J. H. Veitch, the son of J. G., brought over the pink 'Fugenzo' which soon became very popular.

In 1888 there were noticed in some seedlings raised near Welshpool some that looked rather unusual. They were in fact natural hybrids between the Nootka and Monterey cypresses which had been growing close together. It was some years before it was realised that these trees were immensely vigorous, fast-growing and hardy. Now known as Leyland cypress (*Cupressocyparis leylandii*—a Mr. Leyland had raised them) it is an important tree for ornament, hedging and in forestry.

The introduction of the American balsam cottonwood, or poplar (*Populus trichocarpa*) a very rapid growing tree, in 1892, served to augment the range of quick-growing poplars, most of which were hybrids, several with this as a parent and whose increasing cultivation for the purpose of making match sticks and chip-baskets belongs to the twentieth century.

THE TWENTIETH CENTURY

The beginning of the new century saw the first assault by the nursery firm of Veitch on a new part of the world. Russian travellers, French catholic missionaries and a handful of men from our islands (most notably an Irishman, Dr. Augustine Henry) had been studying the natural history of central and western China, whose botanical wealth justifies the word fabulous. In 1899 the firm sent a young man from the mid-lands, E. H. Wilson, who had not before been overseas, to this remote and dangerous area. Thus with Wilson and his successors began an era of plant introduction unequalled before, only ending with the fall of the 'bamboo curtain'.

Many of the trees—maples, rowans, apples and cherries in particular—are gradually taking their place on a considerable scale in our parks, gardens and roadsides. Yet, so far, none has proved of value in our forests.

And as for these forests, their neglect continued, though a number of far-sighted men saw that should war occur our entire dependence on imports would make our existence precarious. There was a need for a national policy, these pioneers said—and they experimented more and more with using the quick growing conifers.

Then in 1914 war came. Submarines cut off our supplies. Our woods and our finest timber trees were devastated. We just scraped through.

The consequence was that a national forest policy was evolved. The Forestry Commission came into being in 1919. To it were transferred all the royal forests except Windsor. Land was acquired and planted. Scientific research into the new problems was carried out. Encouragement and financial assistance were given to private estates.

All was going well when in 1939 war broke out again; in 1945 we had to start once more.

Today, a debtor nation, we import literally millions of pounds worth of timber and timber products such as wood pulp each year, a proportion of which we can produce here. Our woods today are on land that would not otherwise be productive. Their importance in the landscape scene as they begin to mature, though novel, is both satisfying and immense. Their importance in the conservation of wild life of all kinds is vital. The provision of what is called rather vaguely amenity value for a principally urban population is of consequence, too. It must, though, be put in proportion. The growing of trees for timber is and must be the first objective of forestry. The increase in forest fires since the motoring public took to the woods is alarming and may well lead to the closing of them.

The immense variety of trees that we can grow from all parts of the temperate world gives great enjoyment, adding increasing interest and beauty, to our parks, gardens and roadsides. Conifers in general, however, dislike impure air and are little used for street planting.

To deal here with these hundreds of exotics in any detail is out of the question. The commonest kinds are species of maple (*Acer*), whitebeams and rowans (*Sorbus*), cherries (*Prunus*)—which also includes plums, almonds and peaches, crab apples (*Malus*), thorns (*Crataegus*) and the ever popular *Laburnum*.

Forests and woodlands today

As we have seen, for many centuries our natural woodlands have been interfered with by man. Yet the basic, oak-dominated woods still persist; and even when much altered, many of their elements remain, for the oak has evolved around itself a greater and richer ecological association than any other tree.

The major natural oakwood community is 'moist oakwood'. It is found on the heavier soils; it usually has many ferns, the greater woodrush, and numerous mosses. Holly is often present. On account of its fertile terrain, this community has been greatly interfered with.

The 'dry oakwood community' lies on the more sandy and porous soils and on rocky hill sides, where the trees are often dwarfed. Its typical plants include the creeping soft-grass (*Holcus mollis*), bracken and bluebells. Probably owing to its often inaccessible position more of this woodland remains undisturbed.

The oak-birch community is found on still more infertile soils, often on the edge of heathland, and is notable for the high proportion of shrubs that it includes.

There is still much birchwood left, plate 3. The birch is probably the most numerous of all our trees. It will thrive on

25

light soil, and its enormous production of seeds carried by the wind results in the establishment of dense birchwoods when other woodland has been felled, or on ground that otherwise has been cleared. It is not a long-lived tree and, except in infertile situations, is a preliminary stage in the evolution of a more permanent woodland. In England it is not as yet planted by man. The timber is principally used for turnery.

Ash is a common tree, plate 4, also widely dispersed by its winged keys. It is found as an element in most woods, and as pure woods on limestone soils. Its smooth valuable, tough and flexible timber has long been used for the framing of vehicles, and is now popular for sports goods—for example, tennis rackets. There is no better wood for handles and tent pegs.

Beech, though growing over most of our islands, forms quite distinctive woods. The surface root system (quite different in form from that of the oak, which must plunge down deeply) and its tolerance of a high degree of lime in the soil, enables it to thrive on shallow chalk soils such as the Cotswolds, Chilterns and South Downs. There, assisted by foliage formed in dense sheets excluding light, it will suppress all other trees except the yew (which, on rather similar soils, very occasionally forms woods on its own), while few wild flowers are found after early spring. Grey trunks, the fresh green of the leaves in spring and the flaming copper in autumn (the fallen leaves remaining long on the surface of the ground before rotting) make beechwood one of the most distinctive and most beautiful types of our woodland, and one that in every way is a contrast to that of oak. Though a native, most of our beech originates from plantings by man. The timber has long been valued for furniture.

The alder, often growing scattered by the sides of pools and streams, forms woods in a few districts such as in and around Norfolk where they are known as 'carrs'. The timber was used for clogs.

Pinewoods today are principally of two kinds. The Scots pine, native and once preponderant in Scotland (where its timber replaced oak in building structures), has a distinctive flora and beauty. It is rather slow growing but is still planted on light, sandy soil.

In similar conditions—such as the afforestation of Breckland —it has now been largely replaced by the more sombre, quicker growing, straight-trunked Corsican pine, whose timber is perhaps a little inferior.

A third type of wood, as yet not very common, uses the lodge-pole pine, (*Pinus contorta*) which makes coarse growth on good land but does better on poor pine sites than the other two.

Larch woods, large and often small, plate 17, are found principally in hilly districts. The European, Japanese and hybrid kinds are grown; woods of all three are of great beauty when the fresh green leaves break in spring and again when they turn golden before falling; in addition, the twigs of the Japanese larch in winter have a glowing red colour. The timber has, or had, many uses. It is structurally strong, and provided pit props. It was used in ship-building, and is good for joinery.

The Norway spruce is one of the commonest and most adaptable of forest trees on sites that are not unduly exposed and are usually at not too high altitudes. It needs adequate and regular supplies of moisture to thrive. The timber has long been known and has many uses; it is odourless and so is valuable for packing foodstuffs and particularly satisfactory for shredding into wood wool. It is planted with other trees, such as oak, to nurse them up and is grown in great quantities for use as Christmas trees.

The Sitka spruce is the most planted exotic in the British Isles thriving within limitations on poorer soils in areas exposed to wind; it is insistent on a good rainfall, conditions most frequently suited in the west, where it grows rapidly. It provides pit-props, packing case timber and chip-board.

The Douglas fir, the most handsome of our forest-grown conifers, provides the finest, strongest timber of them all. It matures in half the time of oak, but must have reasonably fertile, well-drained soil in protected situations as it is easily thrown over by strong wind.

Other conifers that are increasingly being grown commercially are the western red cedar for its timber of light weight and water-proof qualities and the western hemlock, another tree preferring the moister conditions of the west, and one which can be established under the shade of larger trees.

Locally, the firs *Abies grandis* and *A. procera* are grown, as is, increasingly, the redwood which needs mild and moist conditions. But as yet these three play no great part in our forests.

Of the other trees of economic value, the sweet chestnut is locally important. Large trees seldom provide sound timber —which has all the qualities of oak and is less subject to insect infestation—because they contain 'shakes' which crack. Coppiced every twelve years or so it provides valuable poles used for stakes or cleft into the widely used wire-bound fencing. It was formerly and still is to some extent grown under standard oak. It is chiefly grown in the south-east.

There are still hornbeam woods in the south-east. The timber, as the name implies, is extremely hard and was once used for the cogs in gear wheels. The wood burns with greater heat than any other. Trees were pollarded in careful rotation and the timber used in baker's ovens. It has no economic use now (except, perhaps, for butcher's chopping blocks), but is planted for garden hedges.

In the present century the planting of quick-growing poplars, often grown orchard-wise in comparatively small areas of fertile ground difficult to use otherwise, has become general. The stems are high pruned to produce timber for matches, chip-baskets for fruit and for boxes. Except for *P. serotina* already mentioned, most of the kinds used are hybrids raised comparatively recently in Europe or the United States of America. Growths up to 5 ft. in a year are attained. Experiments are now being made with bigger areas, first growing barley below the young trees, and later, as they reach a good size, laying the land down to grass used for grazing sheep and cattle.

In some districts particularly East Anglia, a form of the white willow with bluish coloured foliage (*Salix alba coerulea*) is grown for cricket bats. The trees are felled when between only 15 and 20 years old.

Fruit trees play an important part in our scenery. Apple, pear, plum and cherry—all are well known. Here recent change in the methods of cultivation is noticeable. Except for cider apples and perry pears the large trees are now being replaced by small ones which come into bearing when quite young; indeed, many are now bushes rather than trees.

The planting of woodlands and their wise and careful management is, apart from their economic value, immensely important from the point of natural conservation and the fertility of our land. We must be careful that economic considerations do not dominate these wider issues.

We must never forget that fine oak grown in the right places and the right way may well in the future be one of our greatest woodland assets.

ODDITIES AND A NOVELTY

We have discussed very briefly those of our native and exotic trees and those introduced from abroad that are usually found in our woods, gardens and parks. We have described them as they grow in nature. Yet a great many trees that are often noticed particularly in urban and suburban districts, in parks, arboreta and pineta—and which catch the eye because of the unusual colour of their foliage or their singular shape—though usually bearing a considerable likeness to the tree already mentioned, are in some respects different.

These—with oddly coloured leaves or rigid, erect or steeply pendulous shoots, for example—play such an important part in the man-made scene that they deserve consideration by anyone interested in trees.

They can all be classified as 'sports'—in the sense of vegetable freaks. These occur at very rare intervals in nature as one isolated example that owing to some peculiarity of its genetical make-up is abnormal in some respect either in its entirety or perhaps only in a branch or group of branches. If such a tree produces seed, then its progeny are usually normal. Consequently the tree having the peculiarity eventually dies and probably no one knows of its existence—it is an abnormality and as such is not encouraged by nature.

Man did not pay much attention to these except perhaps recording them. For instance, a sport of the common hawthorn which produces a few flowers in winter was first mentioned in 1502 as the Glastonbury thorn which, it was claimed had mystical Christian significance.

In general it can be said that in this country we did not bother with propagating these oddities until well on in the eighteenth century. By that time both interest in them among what were well called the 'curious' in the sense of inquiring gardeners and the developments in the techniques of propagation had increased very considerably.

The increase in the number of nurseries propagating trees also, particularly in the nineteenth century, added to the number of these sports, for it seems that they are more liable to arise (and be observed) under artificial conditions. A singular example of this is the Lawson's cypress (*Chamaecyparis lawsoniana*). In nature this tree is consistent in features and is restricted in its natural habitat to a small area of the coastal district from south-west Oregon to north-west California. Very soon after the trees that resulted from the introduction in 1854-55 of seeds and plants to Edinburgh had in turn produced seed, the new generation of seedlings began to produce sports—variations in the colour of foliage, in the form of growth and so on. Less than a century after its introduction 60 of these which had arisen, not only in English but also in foreign nurseries, had been named as distinct and were being propagated. Today, there are some 40 kinds available in the nursery trade.

Of recent years it has become the custom to call these sports which do not come true from seed, cultivars: they are identified in botanical nomenclature by giving the cultivar name with a capital initial, not in italics, in single quotation marks; for example, a silver variegated form of Lawson's cypress is *Chamaecyparis lawsoniana* 'Silver Queen'.

Today, the importance of these cultivars is very great—but surprisingly they are seldom referred to in floras or botanical books. Yet when one realises that few gardens, even quite small ones, are without a Japanese cherry or a flowering crab, nearly all of which trees are cultivars, the tree-lover should surely know something of them. It may be of interest, there-fore, to comment on some of the oldest established and com-monest kinds, type by type.

First, and probably most frequently encountered, are those trees with abnormally coloured leaves, which arise owing to something having occurred in the normal structure of the pigmentation of the leaf. The best known must be the copper, or purple-leaved, beeches, cultivars with different names according to the depth of colour of *Fagus sylvatica*. Red- or reddish-leaved seedlings sometimes appear in nursery seed beds, and no doubt in nature. This fact perhaps accounts for old legends that these red-leaved trees sprang up on the site of where murders, particularly of saints, had been committed. It is said that the first trees cultivated, in the eighteenth century, originated from one in Thuringia—which at least gives us an idea when it came into cultivation.

One of the commonest small purple-leaved trees found in suburban gardens and street planting is a cultivar of *Prunus cerasifera,* the myrobalan or cherry plum, often known as 'Prunus pissardii' but more accurately as *Prunus cerasifera* 'Atropurpurea'. The history of this is well known. A certain Monsieur Pissart discovered it when he was gardener to the Shah of Persia. In 1880 he sent it to Paris, where it was propa-gated and subsequently widely distributed. Other well-known trees that have good red- or purple-leaved forms are the Norway maple (*Acer platanoides*) and several other species of this genus. Red foliage is, however, restricted to few genera; no conifers have it.

Commonest of all colour variations is variegation, that is, green leaves marked with splashes of yellow or silver, or both; sometimes red markings are added. This occurs in many genera, including conifers. One of the first records of a forest tree to have this quality is that of the variegated sycamore, *Acer pseudoplatanus* 'Leopoldii' in which the leaves are marked with cream or white, which was being grown in London in 1730. Another species of maple, the box-elder *Acer negundo,* with leaves more like an ash than most maples, is far more frequently seen in gardens in its cultivar 'Variegatum' than as the natural species introduced here from north-east America in 1688.

Clear yellow-leaved forms are not uncommon. Such is the Corstorphine sycamore, *Acer pseudoplatanus* 'Corstorphinense'. The original tree still grows at that place, near Edinburgh, said to have arisen in 1689. Most of these yellow-leaved trees, however, return to a normal green as the season progresses. One of the most long-lasting and most beautiful is the golden alder, *Alnus incana* 'Aurea'.

Another variation is the cutting up of the leaf margins in an abnormal manner. In the fern-leaved beech (*Fagus sylvatica* 'Laciniata') the leaves are narrow and deeply cut, ending in a sharp point: it is often grown and is a large and most lovely tree. The large-leaved lime has several cut-leaved variants. The Norway maple provides the well-named eagle's claw maple (*Acer platanoides* 'Laciniatum'), the birch *Betula pendula* growing in Sweden has a natural cut-leaved variety, *dalecarlica,* the cut-leaved hornbeam (*Carpinus betulus* 'Incisa') is grown; one occasionally finds cut-leaved branches on normal trees, while the handsome cut-leaved elder (*Sambucus nigra* 'Laciniata') is not uncommon.

The other principal variations from normal in cultivated trees are structural, that is in the formation of the branches.

First is the weeping form. The weeping ash, said to originate from a solitary tree at Gamlingay at Wimpole in Cambridgeshire about 1750 but no doubt having occurred elsewhere, is often seen, having been very popular during the last century. As weeping trees only add height very slowly, if at all, they are grafted or budded high up on the stem of a normal kind. This applies particularly to one cultivar of the popular weeping wych elm, *Ulmus glabra* 'Camperdownii', plate 7. This had an extraordinary origin, being found as a tree sprawling over the ground at Camperdown House near Edinburgh. During the last century it was immensely popular for planting in cemeteries, the shoots falling so vertically that it takes little space. A much more beautiful kind is the wide-growing 'Pendula'.

Many genera of trees produce these exceptional weeping forms: hollies, laburnums, sophora, pears, yews, ginkgos, and, strangest of all, the weeping wellingtonia. One of the most beautiful, and one that is now quite often planted, is the silver-leaved weeping willow pear (*Pyrus salicifolia* 'Pendula'). Some trees have a normal partially weeping form. Such are the silver lime, already mentioned (*Tilia petiolaris*) and two conifers, *Picea smithiana*, the west Himalayan spruce, and the extraordinary, sombre Brewer's spruce, (*P. breweriana*). The weeping willows may be regarded as naturally weeping trees.

Finally come the fastigiate trees, in theory those whose branches grow parallel to the trunk, as in the Lombardy poplar, plate 18. In practice trees with very short upturning branches are included in this category, valuable for planting in restricted areas, such as streets, Among those most commonly seen are the fastigiate forms of the hornbeam (*Carpinus betulus* 'Fastigiata'), hawthorn (*Crataegus monogyna* 'Stricta'), the Dawyck beech, so named from the Scottish estate where it arose (*Fagus sylvatica* 'Fastigiata') and the Wheatley or Guernsey elm (*Ulmus carpinifolia sarniensis*) which makes a tall, flame-shaped tree. Among conifers many gardens have one or another of the popular erect growing forms of Lawson's cypress and the densely columnar Irish yew (*Taxus baccata* 'Fastigiata')—a sport that was found in Fermanagh about 1767—is common in church yards.

Among trees that can be described as naturally appearing to be fastigiate that are not cultivars there is in mild districts the true Italian cypress of the ancients, *Cupressus sempervirens*. The Irish juniper (*Juniperus communis hibernica*) and largest and most dramatic of all, the Californian incense cedar, (*Calocedrus*—or *Libocedrus*—*decurrens*) are hardy.

Finally, there is one important newcomer which, as it is easily propagated from cuttings (and in time should produce fertile seed) is already finding its way into our gardens. Whether it will be a good timber tree is not yet known, though it certainly grows quickly. Trees which are known only as fossils have botanical names comparable with those that still grow on earth. The genus of one of these ancients, preserved (it was thought) only in stone, was called *Metasequoia*. In 1941 a Chinese botanist working in Szechuan province of China discovered a deciduous conifer that he did not recognise. Within a year or two, the tree was identified as being a member of this genus believed to be extinct. Eventually the Americans organised a collection of its seeds, a number of which were sown in this country in 1948, germinating well. The dawn redwood, as it has been called, (botanically it is *Metasequoia glyptostrobiodes*) is very attractive with its fresh green leaves flush in spring that turn pinkish-brown before they fall in late autumn.

32

A COUNTY GUIDE TO SOME OF ENGLAND'S FORESTS, WOODLANDS, ARBORETA AND PINETA

The following list is inevitably selective. It aims to be no more than representative of the some outstanding examples that can be visited by the public.

First, it gives a general idea of the woodland and trees in each county. Next, it gives some details of the major Forestry Commission areas of woodland, particularly those providing facilities for camping, nature study and so on.

Other important national (other than Forestry Commission), local authority, university, National Trust and some private collections that are regularly opened to the public are noted. As opening seasons and dates in some cases vary from year to year, as well as prices of admission, the current issue of *Historic Houses, Castles, and Gardens in Great Britain* (Index Publications, annually) and the list of *Properties of the National Trust* (as amended annually) should be consulted. The lists issued by the Department of the Environment are also useful.

Finally, a number of private properties of interest are noted as opened to the public occasionally at stated times, the openings being in fact for charity. For information concerning these, the annual booklets *Gardens of England and Wales Open to the Public under the National Gardens Scheme* and *Gardens to Visit* issued by the Gardeners' Royal Benevolent Society must be studied. These give precise locations; I have only indicated them approximately.

Very few individual trees of exceptional size or age are mentioned: to embark on this subject would necessitate another volume. Nor can the fascinating question of churchyard yews be discussed here (plate 8): the reader is referred to *The Churchyard Yew and Immortality* by Vaughan Cornish.

It is, I think, a fact that with few exceptions the finest forestry and the finest trees are still to be found in private hands, and not accessible to the general public. It must be stressed that the growing of trees in forests is not primarily one for public amenity and entertainment; it is to provide timber and involves much capital which—like the timber—must not be risked by chance of fire or other damage. Private owners have not the facilities for organising public visits and walks on the scale that is possible with a nation-wide organisation such as is the Forestry Commission.

The visitor or walker in any woodland, park or arboretum

bears a great responsibility not to cause damage or disturb any kind of wild life, nor to leave litter. Most vital of all is to avoid fire—so easily caused, for example, by the dropping of a smouldering cigarette end—which unnecessarily devastates many hundreds of acres each year. If a fire is observed, then the local fire brigade should be telephoned without a moment's delay.

AVON

The county of Avon, except for Avon Gorge itself, is not richly wooded. However, the arboricultural enthusiast will come upon quite a number of interesting trees thriving in this mild climate but it is difficult to attempt any detailed descriptive list.

The woodland most accessible to the most densely populated area around Bristol is the other side of the river Avon where lie the National Trust's Leigh Woods and the Forestry Commission's Bristol Forest; in the latter is the Avon Gorge Forest walk, to which there is a guide. These woods are celebrated for the lime trees and representatives of the genus *Sorbus* (whitebeams and rowans); one, *S. bristoliensis,* is said to be found only in the Avon Gorge. Up to 1942 (when they were felled) there were wild cherries (*Prunus avium*) some 60 ft. tall, girthing 12 ft. and among the biggest in England.

BEDFORDSHIRE

The area of woodland in this county is proportionately small. The Forestry Commission has in Ampthill Forest a fairly considerable area of woodland, with a woodland trail of a novel kind in Maulden Wood east of Ampthill and just north of Clophill.

The most interesting trees in the county are in Woburn Park, for here the Dukes of Bedford have planted trees for centuries. In addition to planting them, the collection was studied and accounts of them published—such as that on the willows, *Salictum Woburnense* in 1831 and on the conifers, *Pinetum Woburnense* in 1839. Luton Hoo at Luton has good trees in the garden and a 'Capability' Brown park. Wrest Park at Silsoe has a large, well-treed garden which has interestingly passed from the old formal canal style to the later landscape manner, examples of both still being present. All these are open at stated times.

BERKSHIRE

The finest and most wide ranging collection of trees in Berkshire is in Windsor Great Park. There are two separate parts. First is the Savill Gardens begun in 1932 by Sir Eric

Savill with his assistant Mr. T. H. Findlay, and with active encouragement from the royal family, particularly King George VI and Queen Elizabeth. Here a rich and varied collection of trees is used as a major element in the design of a remarkable garden which can be classed as one of the great horticultural achievements of the twentieth century. This garden, on the eastern boundary of the park, is enclosed and opened at stated times.

The second area, the Valley Gardens, lies in the park along the north side of Virginia Water. Here are older trees, such as twenty deodar cedars planted about 60 years ago, a pair of monkey puzzles of great height and a beech 109 ft. high. A remarkable sight is a plantation of 200 metasequoias, some the original seedlings. The Pinetum Valley, mostly planted in 1938/9, contains good specimens of some rare kinds. There has been much subsequent planting, including besides conifers numerous birch and nothofagus species. In these Valley Gardens too are many rhododendrons and the spectacular Punch Bowl of dwarf azaleas.

A copiously illustrated account of these gardens and their creation is contained in *The Gardens in the Royal Park at Windsor* by Lanning Roper.

Of commercial forestry, the Crown Estate Woodlands around Windsor and at Bagshot can be observed from the roads in many places and are outstanding examples of good forestry and notable for the fine quality Scots pine which provides many telegraph poles.

The Forestry Commission has no great holding of woodland in the county.

Private gardens with good collections of trees are a feature of the county and a number singled out as such are open on stated occasions under the National Gardens Scheme.

BUCKINGHAMSHIRE

The outstanding woodland feature of this county is the beechwoods principally in the district known as the Chilterns and for long centred on the furniture making town of High Wycombe. The beech has for long been naturally established in this area on the shallow, often chalky soils, and reproduces itself freely. Other forest trees grow well in many parts of the district, but will often be suppressed by the beech with its surface root system not, for example, needing the deeper soil, required by the oak. It was long believed that much of the Chiltern beechwood was ancient. In fact, it was largely increased artificially to supply timber to the developing industry of High Wycombe between about 1720 and 1850. The method of usage was for 'bodgers' to go into the woods and roughly shape the wood for finishing in the factory.

In recent years the bodger has disappeared, and beech of a different type—for example to manufacture plywood—is required. In some places the ground has become 'beech sick'; it seems that the quantity of nitrogenous material is not adequate. Attempts to remedy this include planting foreign species of alder that will tolerate dry ground and build up the nitrogen by means of their root nodules.

In the last twenty years due to changing conditions and a tendency of the beechwoods to deteriorate, they have been carefully studied. One reason for the worsening quality was due to the traditional system of management under which trees were felled with the knowledge that they would be replaced by the natural seedlings that arose in great numbers. What was not appreciated was the fact that it was the good trees, those of fine natural form, that were removed, leaving the inferior trees whose inherited bad qualities began to dominate succeeding generations.

There are many roads and footpaths through the beechwoods from which they may be studied, together with their wild life, particularly botany, which is quite distinct from that of an oak or conifer wood. One of the few other trees found among beeches is the yew, whose evergreen nature enables it to carry out photosynthesis when the leaves of the beech have fallen. The margins of a Chiltern beechwood, on the other hand, are full of variety, comprising those trees (notably the wild cherry or gean) which thrive only on soils with a high lime content.

The Chiltern beechwoods are inevitably and unhappily suffering from the relentless spread of London's dispersal and suburbia as well as from change in those areas where they are deteriorating.

The Forestry Commission has no large forests in this county, but has been responsible for co-ordinating the study into the past, present and future of the beechwoods which are mostly in private hands.

The National Trust has two properties of arboricultural interest. Ascott at Wing near Leighton Buzzard has a number of interesting trees and some unusual topiary. Cliveden, near Maidenhead, also has fine trees, notably an avenue of Atlas cedars, and woodland.

The grounds of Stowe School, near Buckingham, open on stated occasions, are remarkable in showing the development of the English landscape garden from the days of Bridgeman to 'Capability' Brown.

Burnham Beeches is a heavily wooded public open space lying midway between Slough and Beaconsfield owned and managed by the Corporation of the City of London since 1880. Full of interest, its main feature is about 1000 aged beeches which have been pollarded for centuries for firewood. A booklet is available giving details of its history and natural history.

CAMBRIDGESHIRE

This county, which now includes what used to be Huntingdonshire, has a very low proportionate area of woodland; it had no royal forest.

The University Botanic Garden of Cambridge, founded in about 1761 at the centre of Cambridge but moved to a mile away off the Trumpington Road in 1831 though not formally opened until 1845, has a fine collection of trees. There is a Judas Tree (*Cercis siliquastrum*) over a century old covered with its myriads of pink pea-shaped flowers in late May: this species, though coming from southern Europe and western Asia, does very well in Cambridge where it relishes, as do other trees, the dry climate, long hours of sunshine, and alkaline soil. A collection of the trees that grew in Europe before the ice age is another feature.

The National Trust has Anglesey Abbey, north east of Cambridge, with a remarkable garden of about 100 acres on level ground begun in 1930 with fine avenues and many species of trees quite unlike the usual modern woodland garden, having a high degree of formality. It also owns Peckover House in Wisbech on the banks of the river Nene with a small garden including large specimens of the ginkgo and the 'Japanese' pagoda tree (*Sophora japonica*) which incidentally comes from China not Japan. It has leaves like those of a robinia but the small white pea-like flowers open in September. This is another tree that relishes East Anglian sunshine.

In Ely there may be seen overhanging the wall of the Bishop's Palace one of a group of London planes, the largest of which is probably the oldest in England. It was planted by Bishop Gunning between 1647 and 1684.

To an expert the village elms of the Huntingdon area are of considerable interest. It is also known beyond its confines as the area in which the Huntingdon elm originated in a nursery at Brampton a few miles south-west of Huntingdon in perhaps about 1750; this is a hybrid between *U. carpinifolia* and *U. glabra*. It makes a fine shapely tree with a regular, rather rounded crown, and exceptionally large leaves; it is usually botanically known as *U. vegeta*. It is also called the Chichester elm without justification. Today, on account of its fine ornamental qualities, this is quite often planted in avenues and parks. Sadly the famous Huntingdon elm avenue at Hidcote Gardens in Gloucestershire, like many others, can now be seen only on a picture postcard.

There is little Forestry Commission woodland within the county. Elton Hall near Peterborough, opened at stated times, has interesting trees in the beautiful gardens.

CHESHIRE

The county once had extensive woodlands. Lyme Forest on the east (whence Newcastle-under-Lyme in adjoining Stafford-shire got its name) and the Wirral on the west no doubt lost their timber to the salt mines and to industry. The remaining large forest is Delamere. In 1812 an enclosure act was passed giving 8,000 acres to the Crown. This was poor, denuded, sandy ground. On it, as was then the custom, attempts were made to grow oak. This was a failure. Much of the land was turned over to agriculture, the forest crop changing to conifers such as Scots pine which, planted to nurse the oaks, thrived. In 1841 a large supply of deodar seed was received from India and many thousand seedlings went to Delamere in a daring experiment which alas failed. In 1899 Corsican pine was introduced and proved extremely successful. Some areas on the mosses (swampy areas) still remain unsatisfactory for pine which is being replaced by western hemlock (*Tsuga heterophylla*)—an interesting experiment. There is good access to this popular forest, though cars are not allowed on the internal roads.

The National Trust property of Tatton Park (leased to Cheshire County Council) has splendid ornamental trees in the large garden, while the design of the large park was to some extent influenced by Repton.

CORNWALL

This county was formerly much more densely wooded than today. It has two climatic features affecting tree growth: much of it is exposed to very strong winds, in many localities salt-laden, and secondly, the very mild climate. These result in the considerable use of two quick-growing Californian conifers *Pinus radiata* and *Cupressus macrocarpa* coming from the somewhat comparable conditions at Monterey and which are not reliably hardy in much of England being extensively used for shelter. Consequently, too, the most interesting woodland is found in sheltered valleys and coombs.

Cornwall has one most interesting tree that is more or less endemic, being otherwise found only in the neighbouring

Devonshire, and seldom outside that area. It is the Cornish elm known variously as *Ulmus stricta* or *U. carpinifolia cornubiensis*. In it the rather sparse main branching points steeply upwards at first then spreads somewhat to give a narrow crown. It is sometimes mistaken for the commonly planted Wheatley or Guernsey elm, *U. stricta sarniensis* or *U. carpinifolia sarniensis*, a tree with a much finer and more erect-growing branching system.

The main arboricultural interest of Cornwall lies undoubtedly in the number of trees which flourish there on account of the mild climate, along with comparable shrubs.

Though some of the finest collections are not regularly open to the public, excellent examples are to be found in National Trust properties of Trelissick at Feock, south of Truro; Lanhydrock near Bodmin, which has a fine old sycamore avenue and many good trees; and Glendurgan near Mawgan Smith with its remarkable valley running down to the Helford River and richly planted with choice trees.

Most remarkable, indeed unique in the British Isles, is the sub-tropical garden at Tresco Abbey in the Isles of Scilly, open only for stated periods. Here eucalyptus, acacias and many sub-tropical trees abound.

It is interesting to recall that the common trees had their distinctive names in the old Cornish language such as *gwernen*, alder; *bedewen*, birch; *derwen*, oak; and *onen*, ash.

CUMBRIA
(See also Northumberland)

This county includes part of the Border Forest, of which by far the greater area is in Northumberland and described under that county. Its largest constituents are Thornthwaite in the north and Hardknott in the south. These, in the north of the Lake District, are in much more picturesque surroundings than the Kielder country and help to clothe the sides of the hills whose savage bareness was so much disliked in the seventeenth century but so admired by the Victorians; one part of Thornthwaite lies along the side of Bassenthwaite Lake, another is around the Whinlatter Pass. A Forestry Commission booklet, *Britain's Forests—Thornthwaite* (H.M.S.O.), is available.

Hardknott covers a much bigger area and is a National Forest Park. It extends over 7,000 acres and is almost roadless, with spectacular views, and includes the Roman fort of the same name. It is described in *National Forest Park Guide, Hardknott* (H.M.S.O.), which calls it the wildest piece of country now remaining in England.

Another example of pioneering modern forestry, now matured into a scene of great beauty, can be viewed by taking the road round Thirlmere, Manchester's reservoir.

One of the most interesting of all Commission forests is that at Grizedale. It is a compact area of some 7,000 acres of the High Furnace Fells centering on Satterthwaite and lying between Coniston Water and the south of Esthwaite Water. It includes some agricultural land which is run integrally with forestry, and also conducts work on the genetics of trees by forming 'orchards' for controlled seed production.

What is of importance to the visitor is the Wild Life Centre, which includes a 'treetops' observation tower, and the exceptionally interesting Ridding Wood Nature Trail. Here it is possible to study the relations of animals and birds to the forest habitat, a particular study having been made of deer. Pamphlets are available describing the Centre and the Nature Trail.

The National Trust owns much wooded land in the county, a great deal of which is accessible; it is managed both to retain the traditional appearance of the Lake District and to provide soundly run forests.

Levens Hall, near Kendal, is opened at stated times, and has a remarkable topiary garden designed in the style of Le Nôtre at the end of the seventeenth century, though with Victorian replacements. There are fine old lime trees in the park.

Open at stated times are the gardens of Muncaster Castle, overlooking Eskdale, which has good trees, and Holker Hall at Cark-in-Cartmel, with a fine and interesting collection.

DERBYSHIRE

Derbyshire is a county that has much bleak and bare high ground penetrated by dales in which there is delightful woodland. There is much limestone: in the dales, ash is particularly frequent and where it forms cliffs, both species of lime (*Tilia*) and, it now seems, the self-sown hybrid are present: there are references to lime and the 'baisting' of its bark—that is, peeling it off in strips for making ropes, mats and similar articles—in mediaeval documents, when a good deal of the county was under forest law. It is, however, a county of stone, and not timber, buildings. It has considerable areas of woodland, more in private than in Forestry Commission hands. The National Trust owns much property, such as that in the Dove valley, on the Derbyshire—Staffordshire borders north-west of Ashbourne; Longshaw, south-east of Hathersage and Shining Cliff

Wood north of Belper where the typical mixed woodland can be studied.

Of private estates open at stated times, Chatsworth near Bakewell is of outstanding interest. Trees have been planted there for centuries, and since early last century when, under the 3rd ('Bachelor') Duke of Devonshire, Sir Joseph Paxton had charge of the gardens, and subsequently a very great number of conifers and ornamental trees of many kinds have been planted. A guide book is available. Melbourne Hall near Derby has one of the few remaining early eighteenth century formal gardens with paths passing between avenues, and a remarkable yew tunnel known to have been in existence even before the garden was created.

DEVON

There is a great deal for those interested both in ornamental trees and forestry in this county. Historically the only royal forest of any consequence (and from its stony terrain, presumably without much timber) was Dartmoor, which in 1337 passed to the Duchy of Cornwall; red deer were, however, at one time plentiful. From our point of view, its historical importance is that Eggesford Forest, now covering in scattered patches about 1,200 acres, was one of the earliest acquisitions by the Forestry Commission and here, on 8th December 1919 the Commission planted its first trees; these still stand not far from the entrance to the forest from A377 with a memorial plaque beside them. It is a particularly interesting forest; the variety of trees grown is wider than usual. It also displays the development of the trees and the formation and development of the new landscape and its ecology over a long period. In addition there are some of the oldest Douglas fir trees in England. There is a Commission booklet describing the walks within it.

Just north of Exeter are Stoke Woods with walks sponsored by Exeter City Council and the Commission.

On Dartmoor itself, (one of the wettest areas in England) within the National Park, the Commission has several forests: they are well described in Forestry Commission Booklet No. 10 *The New Forests of Dartmoor* (H.M.S.O.) This marks the roads and tracks giving access to the woodlands; there is a leaflet describing the Bellever Forest walk in the woods lying to the south-east of the Yelverton—Moretonhampstead road.

One of the most remarkable oakwoods in England, Wistman's Wood, is on a slope near the West Dart, northwest of Crockern Tor, about 1¼ miles due north of Two Bridges on the Tavistock—Ashburton A384 road. The dwarf oaks, gnarled and fantastic, were poetically described in 1757. They grow among rocks. The trees are of the pedunculate kind whereas in theory they should be sessile. Several ingenious explanations have been adduced as to their origin.

The National Trust has several woodland properties of beauty and interest which are readily accessible, with good paths. Bridford Wood north east of Moretonhampstead and the larger Holne Woods on the banks of the river Dart west of Ashburton consisting of natural oakwoods are among them.

The Trust's property at Killerton, north east of Exeter, a large and one of the oldest woodland gardens, plate 27, begun in the eighteenth century, has superb specimens of conifers, magnolias, eucalypts, immense tulip and other trees that thrive in the mild climate. Saltram House near Plymouth also has fine trees.

The Trust also owns Plym Bridge Woods, north east of Plymouth, covering the wooded valley of the river Plym.

Gardens open to the public at stated times include the remarkable Bicton at East Budleigh which includes a large pinetum with quite exceptional specimens, traversed by a miniature railway, as well as many other fine trees. In all there are something over 230 species to which must be added many of their varieties. There is also the most famous monkey-puzzle avenue in England. Other of the many fine private gardens include Knightshayes Court near Tiverton and Powderham Castle, Kenton, where the cork oaks (*Quercus suber*) are notable.

There are also interesting trees in the public parks in Exeter.

DORSET

This county, it seems, did not play much part under the regime of the old royal forests. The most interesting and largest area owned by the Forestry Commission is Wareham Forest covering over 8,000 acres in separate woodlands stretching from east of Dorchester to west of Poole and from Bere Regis to the sea, with its highest density around Wareham. It is for the most part on poor land, largely on light, acid soil overlaying chalk. Important experiments were carried out here relating to the presence of fungi necessary to the growth of trees. There is much pine, Scots and Corsican, and in the better soils beech. There is a forest walk just north of Wareham itself, and another at Puddletown 5 miles north east of Dorchester. The Commission also has important woodland on Cranborne Chase in the north east of the county where there is also interesting private forestry.

The National Trust has miles of woodland paths on its property Brownsea Island in Poole Harbour.

Of private gardens opened at stated times Abbotsbury (near the famous Chesil Bank) has sub-tropical vegetation with camellias the size of trees. Forde Abbey, near Chard, contrasts modern plantings of trees, including a *Metasequoia* avenue, with its twelfth century building. Minterne, near Cerne Abbas, has many fine and rare trees and is noted for its rhododendrons.

DURHAM

The principal Forestry Commission woodlands in the county are Hamsterley Forest of over 6,000 acres lying in high country mid-way between the river Wear and Teesdale, whose banks are in places richly wooded. Weardale is a smaller forest in the north east of the county.

Open at stated times is Raby Castle, north of Staindrop, which has fine trees, including some good walnuts in the garden.

ESSEX

In Norman times the greater part of Essex was royal forest. By the middle of last century the old forest area had dwindled away. Following the lack of royal interest large areas were enclosed by local landowners and were being lost to the public at an alarming rate. The Corporation of the City of London owned about 200 acres at Wanstead and it was this body, aware of the value of this still open area to Londoners, that after litigation eventually acquired numerous pieces of the old forest land for about £250,000 and opened it, with certain restrictions, to the public in 1882. Epping Forest now covers 6,000 acres in a strip 12 miles long and varying in width between one and two miles wide running roughly north from Wanstead, the site of the once famous (and vast) Wanstead House designed by the architect Colin Campbell early in the eighteenth century and pulled down in 1822. The rest of the forest is typical: much poorish land, heathland, grass—long used for grazing—and ponds. The principal trees are oak, beech, birch and hornbeam with holly, wild apple, field maple and cherry—the oak being on the heavier land. The most interesting of these is the hornbeam, for here it is growing within its natural range. The old trees are usually pollarded (to keep the branch system clear of grazing animals) having for centuries provided firewood and hard timber. Beech was also pollarded. These woods of pollards have a weird, picturesque appearance. Both hornbeam and beech seed themselves naturally. There are very few conifers and few if any are planted. It is thus possible to enjoy and study several distinct types of deciduous woodland of a localised type.

Epping Forest, a useful well-illustrated guidebook with excellent maps, is issued by the Superintendent of the Forest.

The only other remainder of the Essex forest is to be found in the National Trust's Hatfield Forest of 1,000 acres, much of it open land, just east of Bishop's Stortford. Here again pollarded hornbeams are prominent—the pollarding incidentally prolongs the life of a tree; it has been calculated that the oldest of the Hatfield trees are about 300. A remarkable tree is, or was, the Doodle oak, the site of which is recorded. It last bore leaves in 1858—or so it was thought until a few years ago when the late Hon. Maynard Greville found and unearthed the stump, from the roots of which arose a young shoot. He was able to make a calculation which suggested that this remarkable veteran was about 850 years old. The large lake was made in 1760 to help the local unemployed. The National Trust publishes a guide book.

The Department of the Environment owns the great Audley End House near Saffron Walden. This has one of 'Capability' Brown's landscapes with good trees, and the grass is kept short as it would have been originally. Near the dam of the of London planes of different ages showing the variation in river, transformed into a lake, there is an interesting group the foliage of this tree.

At St. Osyth's Priory near Clacton, open on stated occasions, are the remains of the very old Lombardy poplars, planted about 1758 by the Earl of Rochford who brought them from Turin.

GLOUCESTERSHIRE

This county is of exceptional interest to the tree lover. It includes, first, the ancient Royal Forest of Dean, which with its outliers occupies much of the land south of Ross-on-Wye lying between the rivers Wye and Severn now forming a National Forest Park, second, possibly the largest and most imaginatively laid out collection of trees in England at Westonbirt, and third, up on the Cotswolds, beechwoods of exceptional quality.

The Forest of Dean, since 1919 managed by the Forestry Commission in conjunction with the Verderers—a relic of the old system of administering the ancient royal forest and its forest laws, today covers some 27,000 acres, plate 17. In the days when it was first within the forest land it covered 100,000 acres. There are also many acres of woodland—some of extremely good quality—which once formed part of the old forest, in its vicinity still, usually in the hands of private owners. It is mainly situated on a plateau of no great height, traversed by many valleys and undulations, often with streams, of extraordinarily varied geology. One of the larger valleys formerly contained an Anglo-Saxon settlement called Dene, from the Old English *denu* meaning a valley, which eventually gave its name to the whole area.

The complicated geology is the key to the great body of law and custom built up and followed by the courts of the forest. We have the woodland with its timber and deer, and the rights of inhabitants to certain privileges within it, such as the pannage. Then there were the grazing rights on common lands. But exceptional features of Dean were coal, iron ore and valuable stone. The usage of these minerals, except stone, has now largely ceased, and the Commission is planting on the derelict spoil banks.

The history of Dean is well documented both in its written records and visibly on the ground—there are Iron Age remains, the Romans strengthened or opened lines of communication, (it is believed that they first planted the introduced sweet chestnut along them), and the Anglo-Saxons cleared trees for settlements as is indicated by place names. The Normans elaborated and enforced the forest law. They built their castles, notably that of which there are substantial remains at St. Briavels—which town during the thirteenth century was a centre for making 'quarrels', the heavy iron missiles shot by crossbows.

Dean is therefore one of our most interesting forest areas, with several unique features, and one which by means of the new motorways and the Severn bridge is readily accessible to industrial areas as far apart as the midlands and South Wales. Its amenity aspects have been well developed, and include the following features.

Undoubtedly the most spectacular is Symonds Yat rock standing dramatically high and almost vertically above one of the horseshoe bends on the river Wye. A car park, refreshment hut and lavatories are nearby, and are reached by taking a signposted left fork about 1 mile north of Coleford travelling north on B4228. There is a forest walk of singular geological interest passing through a forest garden; excellent explanatory guides are on sale.

In the Forest are also the Christchurch Nature Trail, starting from a Forest Park Camp site south of the Yat, the Speech House Nature Trail—the Speech House, now a hotel, was built in 1680 and includes the Verderer's Court, Cannop Ponds Nature Trail—on wet ground, the Biblins Adventure

Trail south of Symonds Yat and crossing the river, and the Churchill Nature Trail by Park End.

A full illustrated account of the forest, and its natural history, with details of facilities and paths is given in *Dean Forest and Wye Valley, a Forest Park Guide* (H.M.S.O.).

A remarkable and very detailed historical account will be found in *Royal Forest: A History of Dean's Woods as Producers of Timber* by Dr. Cyril Hart, the Forest's Senior Verderer (Clarendon Press, Oxford).

Lying but a few miles north of Dean is the small Dymock Forest, intersected by the M50, a mile and a half south of the small town of Dymock. Within Queen's Wood there is a delightful walk—particularly attractive in spring as wild daffodils abound in the district. The entrance is on the Kempley—Newent road.

The other Gloucestershire woodland of distinguished quality is to be found in the beechwoods, mostly in private hands, but through which many roads, lanes and public footpaths pass. They are probably at their best around Painswick.

A complete contrast is the immense variety of Westonbirt Arboretum. This covers some 160 acres of planted ground. The visitor at once appreciates the fact that this vast collection (still containing some rarities whose names remain in doubt) since it was begun by Robert Holford on open agricultural ground in 1829 has been arranged with a view to displaying the form and colour of the trees to the best advantage not only individually but in respect of one to another. Some of the vistas, now matured, are among the most outstanding examples of garden design using trees that we now have. The fact that it includes hundreds of kinds, many remarkable in flower, foliage and bark, quite unknown to the great landscapers of the past such as Brown and Repton, has brought a new element into garden art.

The site, on fairly level land, has one outstanding and unusual advantage: though much of the arboretum has soil containing lime on which many trees and shrubs, particularly rhododendrons, will not thrive, there is a considerable area of greensand on which they are happy.

Holford began by planting the commoner trees—Scots pines, oaks, evergreen (holm) oaks, cherry, laurel and yew—to provide shelter; many of these are now very fine specimens. Then he laid his plans to give vistas terminating on his house (this, now Westonbirt School, is on the other side of the road and has a fine garden with specimen trees which is open to the public at stated times).

Then came the rarer trees, particularly the new Californians, of which there are many fine specimens, and then Veitch's introductions from Japan. Holford died in 1892 having acquired practically every species of conifer available during the 63 years since he began. For the last 20 years he had been joined by his son, Sir George Holford. In 1876 planting of an additional area, Silkwood, one of old oak and hazel, lying a short way off the main arboretum across a small valley, was begun; here are fewer conifers and more deciduous trees, particularly rare oaks.

Sir George planted with even greater vigour, adding particularly rhododendrons and the many kinds of oriental Japanese maples with their brilliant autumn colour. At the beginning of the next century the wealth of western and central China was coming to England—snake-bark maples whose green bark was striated with white patterns, the remarkable *Acer griseum* whose copper bark peels off like sheets of paper; the dove tree (*Davidia involucrata*) whose giant white 'flowers' (in reality the bracts that enclose them) do look like a flight of doves (the unromantic call them handkerchiefs) perching on the tree; a whole host of rowans, of which *Sorbus sargentiana,* is the most remarkable, with shoots and buds like those of a horse-chestnut, scarlet berries and flaming autumn leaves. There are, too a number of Chinese conifers, such as the spruce, *Picea brachytyla,* whose leaves are bluish-white underneath.

Sir George died in 1926, and was succeeded by Lord Morley. The curator, W. J. Mitchell continued to plant, his great work being commemorated in the Mitchell Drive and the lovely *Sorbus mitchellii.*

Lord Morley died in 1951 and the future of the collection was in some doubt until 1956 when the Forestry Commission took it over.

Today, there are some 2,000 specimens of about 500 species of trees, with many shrubs. There is no day in the year when something is not seen of interest and to give pleasure. The arboretum is a remarkable example of the great number of exotic trees to which the British Isles gives hospitality. Autumn colour is at its most brilliant at mid-October.

An excellent booklet, *Westonbirt in Colour* by A. F. Mitchell (H.M.S.O.) is available.

The arboretum is $3\frac{1}{2}$ miles south west of Tetbury on the A433 road.

There are also some good trees in Hidcote Manor Garden (National Trust) at Hidcote Bartrim 4 miles north east of Chipping Campden; particular note should be taken of the avenues.

Batsford Park, 1½ miles north west of Moreton-in-Marsh, occasionally opened on stated dates, is of great arboricultural interest. The planting was begun by Lord Redesdale last century, and contains many interesting, now mature trees, particularly from Japan to which he was ambassador. It has been greatly and most interestingly increased during recent years by Lord Dulverton.

GREATER LONDON

Within the heart of London an immense variety of trees is to be found. Two kinds are particularly associated with it, the most famous being the London plane (*Platanus hybrida* or *acerifolia*), plate 15. This is a relative newcomer; the *Gentleman's Magazine* of 1765 remarked on its novelty, though referring to one or two good specimens, and observing that it stood town conditions well. Possibly the trees in Berkeley Square, planted in 1789, are now the oldest. Extensive planting did not begin until about 1811 in conjunction with developments with which the architect John Nash was associated; it has been estimated that 60 per cent of the trees in London are this plane.

The other tree that stands out, particularly in July and early August when its exotic-looking flowers open (to be followed by fruits like runner beans), is the catalpa. How different is the churchyard of St. James in Piccadilly, or the Victoria Embankment Gardens and many other places where it thrives, from the riversides of Georgia and Florida whence it was brought in 1726 (the legend that Sir Walter Raleigh introduced it must be disregarded).

There is no arboricultural subject of greater interest than the trees in the London parks, both to visitors and to those who can follow their progress daily. Yet the only book in existence by A. D. Webster is over half a century old. He names many species which then did well in the central districts —there are now probably more. Conifers and evergreens such as holly are in general not happy, but an exception is the strawberry tree (*Arbutus unedo*).

Webster counted two hundred and twenty distinct kinds growing in Kensington Gardens and Hyde Park alone. Unfortunately, today practically none are labelled and on many the leaves are out of reach to enable identification to be made: a visit in autumn when the leaves are falling is helpful. To attempt any description of the trees that are growing here is impossible, but indications of the most interesting areas for discovery follow.

1. The angular pedunculate oak (Quercus robur) at Bodiam Castle, Sussex.
2. The clean growing sessile or durmast oak (Quercus petraea) grown for timber.

3. Birch (Betula ver-
rucosa) self-seeded
at wood edge.

4. Ash (Fraxinus ex-
celsior): a neglected
coppiced tree.

5. Rowan (Sorbus aucuparia) in typical heathland situation.

6. Solitary hawthorn (Crataegus monogyna), Sutton Park, West Midlands.

7. Wych elm (Ulmus glabra): weeping form 'Pendula', Staffordshire.

8. Yew *(Taxus baccata)* in Much Marcle churchyard, Herefordshire.

9. Weeping beech *(Fagus sylvatica 'Pendula')*.

10. *Bole of hornbeam (Carpinus betulus) showing fluting and roughness distinguishing it from smoothness of beech.*

11. *Hedgerow elm (Ulmus pro-cera).*

12. Sycamores (Acer pseudoplatanus) protecting farm buildings on Derbyshire moors.

13. Sweet chestnut (Castanea sativa): ancient specimen at Bewdley, Worcestershire.

14. European lime (Tilia europaea), Clumber Park, Nottingham-shire.

15. The bark of London plane (Platanus hybrida), Kensington Gardens.

16. Oriental plane (*Platanus orientalis*), Weston Park, Salop.

17. European larch (*Larix decidua*) on left, Norway spruce (*Picea abies*) on right, in spring in the Forest of Dean.

18. (above). The fastigiate
Lombardy poplar
(Populus nigra italica).

19. (below). The very large and handsome leaves of the tree of
heaven (Ailanthus
altissima), Kensington
Gardens.

20. The wellingtonia, the most massive tree in the world
(Sequoiadendron giganteum).

21. The stone pi
(Pinus pinea,
Kew.

22. The South
American
monkey puzzle
(Araucaria
araucana), at
Dropmore, Bucks.

23. *Atlas cedar (Cedrus atlantica) at Eastnor Castle, Herefordshire.*

24. The Lebanon cedar (Cedrus libani).

25. An ancient pagoda tree (Sophora japonica) in England's first botanic garden —Oxford.

26. Kew Botanic Gardens — a swamp cypress (Taxodium distichum).

27. Killerton Gardens, Exeter, cork oak and eucalyptus.

28. An incense cedar (Calocedrus decurrens).

29. Our largest modern forest, Kielder, Northumberland.

Entering Kensington Gardens by the Marlborough Gate (nearly opposite Lancaster Gate Underground station) a right turn along the walk parallel to Bayswater Road passes a great variety. Turning left by Lancaster Gate and walking towards the bridge over the Serpentine a number of other kinds stand out among the predominant planes, which may be examined by taking a zig-zag route, occasionally touching the bank of the Serpentine itself where there is a fine deciduous cypress (*Taxodium*). From the bridge itself in late September may be seen the large white spikes of the handsome evergreen tree privet, *Ligustrum lucidum*. But one must now walk back towards the Alexandra Gate until the Flower Walk is reached, so well named and containing sufficient of interest to traverse its length first examining what is on its left, then at its end, returning and studying the other side—where one will notice the evergreen Californian laurel (*Umbellularia californica*), often called the headache tree because rubbing the aromatic leaves or even standing underneath it gives some people an allergic headache: I have never noticed that this affects the Londoners almost always sitting under it! Following a return to the east end of the Flower Walk, Hyde Park is entered and a walk taken alongside Rotten Row. The once famous elms are no more. At the broad east end of the Serpentine turn into the Dell—where again other interesting trees can be spotted. This walk is one that I have repeated at all seasons for many years, and I can recall no occasion on which I have not noticed an interesting tree for the first time.

There are good trees in the Green Park also, while St. James's Park has even greater variety: by the bridge over the lake is a large fig-tree—growing literally as a tree and not, as is usually the case, trained to a wall.

Regent's Park, with its remarkable collections of plants, is just as full of interest: it contains a good number of the more recent introductions, particularly the flowering cherries. Battersea Park and Holland Park must not be missed either.

An historical account of Kensington Gardens will be found in the then Ministry of Works Report *Trees in Kensington Gardens* (1959) published by H.M.S.O.

On London's outskirts Greenwich Park, Hampton Court and Bushy Park are famed for their magnificent avenues, all of which had their origins in the seventeenth century designs, either just after the Restoration in the case of Greenwich, or of the great radiating design at Hampton Court during the reign of William and Mary. Greenwich has notable old chestnuts (*Castanea*). Bushy, adjoining Hampton Court, has the famous horse-chestnut avenue—though this tree was in fact placed within outer lines of European limes. When a survey was made of the Bushy avenue from Hampton Court Gate to Teddington Gate in 1963 there were still a number of horse-chestnuts remaining that were planted in 1699.

The history, present states and future treatment of the trees in these royal parks is fully described in two Department of of the Environment reports, *Trees in Greenwich Park* (1964) and *Trees in Hampton Court and Bushy Parks* (1963) published by H.M.S.O.

Syon House, Brentford, with its Garden Centre, open at stated times, has been famous for its trees since the sixteenth century and is set in a 'Capability' Brown landscape.

Also regularly opened is Hogarth's House, Chiswick which has the artist's mulberry tree still surviving after serious damage by a German bomb.

The Royal Botanic Gardens at Kew actively began its history as a botanic garden in about 1751 on the site of an already famous garden at Kew House. Except for one or two unhappy periods it has been developing and adding to its collections ever since. It was one of the first gardens to organise plant collection overseas. So far as the trees are concerned, it is today the oldest and probably the most complete collection in England, though on a soil and in an impure air that are far from satisfactory—particularly for conifers, plate 26. One of the first important accessions was after the death of the 3rd Duke of Argyll in 1761 who at Whitton near Hounslow had been collecting trees, particularly the new kinds then being introduced, since about 1720. Fine specimens, both ancient and young, are scattered all over the garden and collections arranged genera by genera are established. Their areas, to the west and south, are shown in a guide published by H.M.S.O. available at the entrances. A much fuller account by W. B. Turrill is the *Royal Botanic Gardens, Kew, Past and Present*.

Richmond Park, just south of Kew, is of course a wonderful sanctuary of wild life and has many fine trees and plantations.

Nor should the tree enthusiast forget that there is much to be learned in the galleries of the British Museum, (Natural History) in the Cromwell Road, Kensington.

HAMPSHIRE AND THE ISLE OF WIGHT

The dominating woodland interest of Hampshire, indeed one of the outstanding in England, is the New Forest. Today, one of the largest areas of unenclosed land in England, its history and many of its particular features can be linked with and are in some respects continued from Norman and even pre-Norman days. Lying between Southampton and the Hampshire Avon, the New Forest Perambulation of 1964 covered an area of about 145 square miles. Of this some 40 square miles, including land adjoining the Solent, are in private hands. The remaining 105 square miles are in public ownership, under the Crown, and there is public access to most of it.

The land seldom rises to any great height above sea-level, 400 ft. or so is the highest. It consists of dry, sandy heath, rather poor land carrying few trees, with grazing in some parts —occasionally Scots pines are naturalized—and richer lower lying, well drained land on which trees grow well—particularly oak, beech, yew, holly and thorn: here more valuable conifers are planted. Finally there are areas of marshland where the predominant trees are alders and willows.

It is an area for the most part unsuited to agriculture and, unlike Dean Forest, without minerals. The absence of local stone or brickfields prevented much building until during the last century, when it became a fashionable district for gentlemen's residences.

The New Forest was, therefore, an ideal place for the hunting of deer and the growing of timber, particularly oak which was readily accessible to ship builders nearby. Very considerable plantations were made in the opening years of the nineteenth century to produce the open grown, spreading and angular timber for the framing of our 'wooden walls'. By the time it matured, steam and steel had replaced sail and timber.

It is an interesting fact that the first differentiation of the two species of oak found in England originated in the New Forest. In 1791 T. Nichols published a book called *Observations on Oak Trees*. In it he wrote "There are two different kinds of oak growing in the New Forest, one the true English . . . the other called by woodmen in the forest durmast oak." It seems clear that the foresters and no doubt shipwrights had long ago discovered the qualities of timber of the two kinds— for their purposes in those days preferring the angular tougher pedunculate kind (*Quercus robur*) to the cleaner growing sessile (*Q. petraea*). The origin of the woodman's name of durmast is a mystery: there is still a place of that name in the forest which in early times was remote and was no doubt where this kind grew.

Today there is no place in England of such easy access where woodland and woodland life of all kinds may be studied. They range from old untouched areas, which are much the same today as they were on that fateful August 2nd 1100

67

when Sir Walter Tyrell either by chance or purpose killed William Rufus (Ocknell Pond still runs red where Tyrell washed the blood from his hands), to all types of modern forestry and land usage.

There are two interesting arboreta. The Bolderwood Arboretum was begun in 1860 and has some modern additions; by it is the Rhinefield Ornamental Drive originating in 1859; both are in the area running north west from Brockenhurst, crossing A35 and ending near A31. Forestry Commission guide books are available for each.

The administrative centre of the forest has for long been the Queen's (or, when a king is on the throne, King's) House in Lyndhurst. It dates mainly from the time of Charles II.

An excellent *Forestry Commission Guide to the New Forest* (H.M.S.O.) is published. It discusses its history, wild life of all kinds, geology and present forestry activities, and gives routes for walks, details of camping sites, etc.

There are other important forests in Hampshire. Bere Forest is across Southampton Water from the New Forest. Lying to the north of the Portsdown Hills, in 1688 it covered about 16,000 acres. It is now a Forestry Commission forest, with a forest walk near Wickham.

There is much other woodland, both Commission and private, in Hampshire; it is the third most densely wooded county in England.

The National Trust property of Mottisfont Abbey, north west of Romsey, has one of the largest London planes (*P. hybrida*) in England. The Trust also owns Selborne Hill and has under covenant the area south of Alton made famous by Gilbert White in his *Natural History of Selborne,* with its beechwoods.

Open at stated times are the Exbury Gardens, made famous by the late Lionel de Rothschild with the azaleas and rhododendrons he raised. In this considerable area of wonderful woodland garden, which is south of the New Forest overlooking the Solent and between the Beaulieu River and Southampton Water and thus has an exceptionally temperate climate, are fine trees of many kinds, some rare, both old and new.

There are Forestry Commission woods in the Isle of Wight. There is a guide to the Brighstone Forest Trail on an area of chalk downland. This is interesting in that it is planned eventually to be a beechwood. In certain places the effects of exposure to sea winds can be seen.

HEREFORD AND WORCESTER

The old county of Hereford still contains a higher proportion of valuable oak and ash timber than any other. It has
some of the tallest and largest girthed oaks in the country, one
reaching 136 ft, though the top was damaged by lightning
some years ago. In other private woodlands there are stands
of oak whose acorns are regularly collected by the Forestry
Commission to ensure continuity of such valuable strains.

The fertile lower lands are given over to farming, notably
cattle, fruit and hops, while forestry is carried out on the
many hills, which though of no great height are, however,
stony, often somewhat steep, and difficult to work.

A good example is the Commission's big Haugh Wood on
the Woolhope Hills in which there is a nature trail not far
from the village of Woolhope on the road to Mordiford. An
ancient oak forest, it was reputedly the home of a dragon which
drank from the river at Mordiford; much of it has been replanted in recent decades.

The other big woodland, also the Commission's, is Mortimer
Forest, lying north west of Mortimer's Cross. This reaches
up to south-west Salop (which see) and has some very fine
timber, notably Douglas fir. It is steeply hilly with many
fine views. The river Lugg (meaning 'shining river') cuts its
way through, and there are many delightful lanes passing
through the trees.

On the Welsh border in the north the land becomes poorer,
and the trees are less luxurious.

The banks of the Wye below Hereford, particularly in the
places where they are steep and stony, are of considerable
interest. Several species of sorbus are found. Caplar Wood,
on a very steep bank immediately above the Wye, is famous
for its large and small-leaved lime. A footpath not far from
Fownhope church runs beside it.

The lower reaches of the Wye divide Gwent (lying on the
west) and Gloucestershire with outlying parts of Dean Forest
on the east.

There are two exceptional private collections of trees which
are open to the public at stated times. On the Ledbury-Tewkes-
bury road (A430) some 2 miles east of Ledbury, among the
foothills of the Malverns, is the great, early nineteenth century
pile of Eastnor Castle. Mainly during Queen Victoria's reign
ornamental trees, particularly conifers, were planted immediately around the castle, spreading out into the adjoining park
land. It was here about 1845 that the second Earl Somers raised
seedlings of the Atlas cedar (*Cedrus atlantica*), plate 23, from
cones that he had collected in its native habitat Téniet-el-Hâad.

It is believed that these were the first ever grown in the British Isles. Today, with their progeny, they make the finest collection of these magnificent trees in the country. The range of their colouring—some are quite silver—is remarkable. There are also superb deodars, Lebanon cedars, incense cedars (*Calocedrus* or *Libocedrus*), *Abies nobilis,* some good *Tsugas,* a big bishop's pine, (*Pinus muricata*) with prickly cones that remain unopened on the tree almost, it seems, indefinitely, and good examples of later Japanese introductions. The most magnificent of all the trees are two specimens of the extremely rare Santa Lucia fir (*Abies bracteata* or *venusta*), from the Santa Lucia mountains in California. One, the largest in the country, planted out in about 1863, is now more than 117 ft. high. This remarkable tree is easily distinguished by its large, sharply-pointed leaves two or more inches long and buds like those of a beech but larger; the cones are covered with long, whiskery bracts.

In the park is one of the few oak trees bearing mistletoe, while it is believed that the sessile oakwoods on the Malverns above the park and around the hamlet of White-leaved Oak are the direct descendants of our primeval oak forest.

The other outstanding collection of trees is at Hergest Croft and the closely adjoining Park Wood. Lying just off the A44 road west of Kington, it is in many ways a contrast to Eastnor, having been begun at the end of the last century and containing in particular some of the now finest examples of the trees from Western China introduced by E. H. Wilson and his successors. The whole place in spring and early summer glows with the rhododendrons and azaleas which grow beneath them. The most remarkable features are the Asiatic birches with remarkable coloured trunks and the Chinese maples, including a huge paper-bark maple *Acer griseum.* In Park Wood is one of the few specimens in this country of *Acer giraldii* which carries leaves up to nine and more inches across. There are many other maples and some exceptionally beautiful conifers.

The county owns an area of woodland (from which fine views are seen) on the top of the landmark, Dinmore Hill. In part of this a large collection of ornamental trees has been established, which is now becoming most decorative. Planting continues steadily. Named the Queenswood, it lies against the western side of the A49, some 8 miles north of Hereford and 5 miles south of Leominster. It is permanently open.

'Capability' Brown's Berrington Hall, laid out in 1780 and lying 3 miles north of Leominster on the west of A49, is a National Trust property with fine old plantings.

At Croft Castle, signposted from the Ludlow—Leominster

road (A49) and at Mortimer's Cross on A4110, is probably the finest and oldest sweet chestnut avenue in England, as well as other good trees.

The major wooded area of the old county of Worcestershire is Wyre Forest, running along the western side of the Severn from Bewdley northwards for some miles and spreading westward to Cleobury Mortimer; it is the remains of dense woodland shown on the Ordnance Survey Roman map covering the whole of north-western Worcestershire; there are, in fact, many smaller areas of woodland still surviving beyond its confines. In A.D. 816 the district was known as *Weagorena leage,* the woodland of the Wigoran tribe; by 904 we find Worcester described at Wigrecaster, the Roman fort of the tribe called the Wigoran. The woodland, therefore, gave its name to the county. For long it was in the hands of the powerful Mortimer family. Today the woodland area consists of some 6,000 acres of which the Forestry Commission has since 1925 acquired some 2,600 acres.

It was for centuries a natural oak forest growing fine timber until about the time of the accession of Queen Elizabeth I when it was largely managed as oak coppice to provide charcoal for the nearby iron founding, bark for tanning, and small timber for fuel. There have long been and still are small timber-using industries in the district, producing for example rustic work for gardens in the nearby housing estates.

In the main area now owned by the Commission there are some good forest roads and tracks from which it is possible to see areas of the old type of coppiced oak woodland, the stems now grown tall and picturesque, as well as districts now replanted, particularly with some good Douglas fir. There is a great deal of wild, particularly bird, life to be seen. The botany is also interesting, and there are deer. The entrance to the car park is near the forestry buildings to the north of A456 at Callow Hill about 2 miles west of Bewdley. A guide to the woodland walks is available. This mentions a remarkable tree that was discovered in the forest in 1678, locally known as the whitty pear. It was the European service tree (*Sorbus domestica*), not a native of England and believed to be the only one ever to have been found wild in our country. It was most probably planted two or more centuries before that—precisely when, or why or by whom remains a mystery. It is the first recorded instance of the tree being observed in England. The original tree lived until 1862; that now seen is a direct descendant of the original.

Adjoining Birmingham (which owns it), though in Worcestershire, is the splendid public open space surrounding the Lickey

Hills. There is much attractive woodland, with a network of paths, which enables a study to be made of all the common natives as well as most of the conifers normally used in forestry. There are also a number of ornamental trees. The main access is from the Rednal bus terminus in Lickey Road.

Nearer to the industrial Black Country are the Clent Hills, a National Trust property, with some interesting woodland open to the public. This area adjoins Hagley Hall, and can be reached by a footpath across Hagley Park (passing Hagley church) from A456. This traverses one of the first landscape gardens ever made in this country. It was created by George, later first Lord, Lyttelton, from about 1747 onward; some of the original trees still remain.

The gardens of Spetchley Park, just east of Worcester on the Stratford (A422) road, open at stated times, contain some very interesting specimens.

During the Three Counties show (usually held in mid-June) there is an interesting woodland walk in Langdale Wood adjoining the show ground at Malvern.

HERTFORDSHIRE

The western boundary of the county is typical Chiltern country with shallow and chalky soil. Beech is a common tree, as is the wych elm. Eastwards, the heart of the county is predominantly agricultural and southwards it becomes suburban, then urban and industrial, with the consequent destruction of old estates and fine trees. The common hedgerow elm tends to disappear from the scene to be replaced by the smooth-leaved elm in its varying forms. The hornbeam is found as in indigenous tree.

Trees and woodland can be seen on the National Trust's large Ashridge property, varied in its type of land and spreading into Buckinghamshire and Bedfordshire. It lies north of Berkhamsted. The spacious grounds of Ashridge House itself (not Trust property) are open on stated occasions and include some notable trees and avenues. Fine trees are to be seen at Hatfield House, including some aged avenues and, in the gardens, what may well be the remains of the oldest extant mulberry trees in England.

KENT
(see also Surrey and Sussex)

Kent is a richly wooded county; with Surrey and Sussex and the east of Hampshire it was in early times the *Sylva Anderida* of the Romans and *Andredswald* of the Anglo-Saxons. At that time it is said to have been an area of dense

woodland 120 miles long and 30 miles deep, described by
Bede in the eighth century as thick and inaccessible, the abode
of deer, swine and wolves. It had since about 450 B.C. been
the home of the iron smelting industry and continued to be
so until the eighteenth century (see *Sussex*). The whole area
is admirably dealt with in C. A. Barrington's *Forestry in the
Weald* (Forestry Commission Booklet No. 22) H.M.S.O.

Traces of the old woods, such of those in Ashdown, are
often found and, in addition to some large modern forests,
the county is freely scattered with many delightful small woods.
Much coppiced chestnut is grown—formerly it was used in
the hop-yards.

The Forestry Commission has a number of forests with
walks. These include Joyden's Wood in Shipbourne Forest in
the nearest Commission woodland to London—fourteen miles
from Charing Cross and one from Bexley Station! Challock
Forest is the biggest in Kent, covering almost 5,000 scattered
acres. King's Wood walk is 5 miles north from Ashford on
the Faversham road. Clowes Wood walk is 4 miles south east
of Whitstable. Lyminge Forest walk is 7 miles due north of
Hythe. Dene Park walk is 3 miles north-north-east of Ton-
bridge.

In the southern part of Kent, there is a walk in Orlestone
Forest, lying 5 miles south of Ashford. Vinehall, Footland
Wood walk is at Cripps Corner about 2 miles south east of
Robertsbridge.

For those wanting to learn about conifers, the most important place to visit is the Commission's Bedgebury Pinetum, 2
miles south of Goudhurst. It was begun as recently as 1925
by the late William Dallimore on a 64 acre site of the old
Bedgebury Forest. The situation is far from ideal for trees
in many ways, but makes attractive settings for them, being
undulating, with springs, streams and a lake. Although primarily scientific with the different genera grouped together, the
pinetum is already a place of great beauty, as fortunately
Dallimore had a natural genius for design. The most beautiful
and perhaps, particularly for a gardener, the most interesting
part is the cypress valley where grow the true cypresses
(*Cupressus*) and the 'false' cypresses (*Chamaecyparis*) both as
species and in their multitudinous garden forms. Other attractive features are the swamp cypresses (*Taxodium*) growing by
the lake, together with dawn redwoods (*Metasequoia*).

Across the road are experimental forest plots of trees (not
only conifers) that are not normally grown in forestry.

There are many private gardens in Kent with fine or interesting trees or in which trees are used with great effect. Among

those open at stated intervals are Chilham Castle near Canterbury; Cobham Hall near Rochester; Hever Castle near Edenbridge; Penshurst Place, Tunbridge Wells; Scotney Castle, near Lamberhurst; and Sissinghurst Place (not Castle) near Cranbrook.

LANCASHIRE AND GREATER MANCHESTER

This county has only a small percentage of its area under woodland—much of it is of an industrial type that is destructive to the growth of trees and inevitably the exceptionally long coast line is particularly bare. Bowland Forest stands out as a considerable area on the map and it was in early times only one part of the large forest covering north east Lancashire and running into Yorkshire called Blackburnshire; the Forestry Commission still have some 5,000 acres there. There are remarkable old trees in the strangely named Trough of Bowland.

One feature of the flat land of the west of the county is the frequent use of the grey poplar (*P. canescens*) as a shelter tree in groups and in hedgerows; it is usually bent over by the persistent, battering wind from the sea.

Another singular local tree is known as the Manchester poplar, in which city (where ten years ago half of the trees were this kind) and a few other northern towns it has been over planted. It is a variant of our native black poplar (*Populus nigra betulifolia*) which has a narrow, erect crown when young which becomes spreading and carried on a crooked stem when middle aged; it will, however, thrive in the poisoned air.

LEICESTERSHIRE

Leicestershire is among the counties with least woodland, though the name Charnwood Forest, to the north west of Leicester, is prominent on maps. In fact it appears never to have been a royal forest, though still a picturesque area of hilly country, wooded in places, with distinctive rocky outcrops. Aspects of the Charnwood scenery are little changed since Michael Drayton wrote of it in his *Polyolbion* in 1622. It may be well viewed from the numerous roads that traverse it, though most of the land is privately owned and inaccessible to the public; these roads are usually well and thoughtfully planted with trees.

Bradgate Park, an old deer park of 1250 acres on the south east of the forest and but a mile or so from the outskirts of Leicester itself, is one of the few areas in the county that has never been cultivated; it is now owned by local authorities and open to the public.

Leicestershire is unfortunately one of those counties in which field hedges and their timber are, it appears, unwisely considered to be inimicable to agriculture and have too often been removed.

There was at one time forest in the southern part of the former county of Rutland, now taken over by Leicestershire, but by the seventeenth century it had diminished greatly. There is evidence that lime trees were growing in it during medieval times. The Forestry Commission's Kesteven Forest in Lincolnshire spreads into Rutland.

LINCOLNSHIRE

This county has a low proportion of its land under timber. The wolds and fens are not ideal terrain for tree growing. It is interesting to note that this appears to have been so in medieval times as there are records of timber being carried down the Trent from the midlands and Sherwood to build Lincolnshire churches.

There are some fine park trees and avenues, as for example at the National Trust's Gunby Hall, Burgh-le-Marsh; at Belton House, Grantham; and at Doddington Hall south west of Lincoln; all of which are open at stated times.

NORFOLK

Norfolk includes three distinct and interesting areas. In the west are the fens, skilfully drained by man, and with little ground covered by trees. In the east are the broads with the very distinctive vegetation of the 'carrs' on which alder grows and becomes dominant.

From the forester's point of view the most interesting district in the south-west of the county running into Suffolk (under which it is also mentioned) is called Breckland. It is the driest area of England and is subject to severe frosts in summer. Geologically it is chalk overlaid by sand, which has suffered from wind erosion. It covers more than 400 square miles of undulating country, most of which long remained uncultivated, the principal product being the rabbits that abounded. In places there were trees, particularly birches and pines.

The centre of this area is Thetford, for long a small country town but recently turned into an industrial community. And the sterile area of Breckland surrounding it has, since the early days of the Forestry Commission, been turned into Thetford Chase, covering upwards of 50,000 acres. It is mostly pine, Corsican being predominant. The large plantations on the undulating ground form a series of banks or ridges, and the effect now the trees have grown is rather like huge sea waves piling one on another. There are many delightful open glades of the old trees by the sides of the main roads passing through the forest, in which there are two marked walks, the King's Forest walk starting from West Stow and Santon Downham Forest walk. A feature of Thetford is that the red squirrel, in most of England ousted by the imported grey squirrel, is so happy among the pines that it has returned to the district and is now dominant.

There are other areas of interesting woodland. About 7 miles south west of Fakenham roads run through the Weasenham woodland developed by the Coke family following a system of mixed forestry using a variety of species—a very different type of silviculture from that of the Forestry Commission.

The National Trust property of Blickling Hall near Aylsham has much woodland accessible to the public. The fine rather formal garden also has some good trees, the most interesting of which is a group of oriental planes some of which, as so often happens with this tree, have huge lower branches lying on and probably layered in the ground. The curving lake and the clever planting of trees around it which greatly enhances its apparent size are splendid examples of eighteenth century landscaping, the designer of which is apparently unknown.

Holkham Hall, near Wells, open at stated times, was created by the first Earl of Leicester on a site which was principally barren heath and saltmarsh, the fine house by William Kent being started in 1734. The now richly wooded situation—there are for example superb ilexes—is the work of him and his successors, an early example of land reclamation. The second Earl of Leicester in about 1860 reclaimed six hundred acres from the sea and planted, to protect the land, the Corsican pines that stretch from Wells to Burnham Overy. The trees have since spread naturally on the sandy seaward side.

NORTHAMPTONSHIRE

In medieval times Rockingham in the north of this county was one of the great royal forests, William I having built the original castle at that place standing high above the surrounding land. It is now largely an Elizabethan building within the old castle wall, with remarkable yew hedges. The area was finally disafforested at the end of the eighteenth century, much of it already by then being in private hands. The Forestry Commission still has its scattered Rockingham Forest of over 6,000 acres in the district lying south-east of the castle. Whittlebury Forest was in the centre of the county.

The present Salcey Forest, formerly royal, now Forestry

Commission, lies on the east of M1 about 8 miles south east of Northampton. Not far away it has woodland at Yardley Chase, spreading into Buckingham and Bedfordshire.

There are finely timbered parks in the county, some of which are open on stated occasions. Althorp, north west of Northampton, has very fine old trees particularly in its oak avenues. Castle Ashby, east of Northampton and north of Yardley Chase, also has good trees.

In a number of places where extensive digging for iron-stone has wrecked the landscape, as around the modern steel town of Corby (which was originally within the bounds of Rockingham Forest) extensive and interesting planting of trees has been done. Whether it will succeed remains to be seen.

NORTHUMBERLAND
(see also Cumbria)

This county provides, with its neighbouring Cumbria and adjoining Scotland, the most remarkable modern forestry undertaking in England. Within it, the Forestry Commission owns a total of over 133,000 acres of land (which includes that left for grazing) which in 1920 was practically treeless. In Cumbria the area is less, some 21,000 acres, while in adjoining Scotland another 20,000 acres is held. The whole of this area of a great new forestry venture, is described as a whole in *The Border,* a National Forest Park Guide (H.M.S.O.).

The largest unit is the huge Kielder Forest, plate 29, a remote and inaccessible area, mostly giving one a feeling of being high up in what would have been a barren area hostile to man if it were not that he is conquering its enmity with his trees—mostly spruces. Through its heart winds the beautiful river North Tyne—so different from its descendant down by Newcastle!

The centre of the Forest is at Kielder Castle, from which a guide map can be obtained, also details of the Lewisburn and Kielder Castle Forest Trails. It must be emphasised that it is a remote and sparsely inhabited district, of great general and natural interest, and exceptional as being England's biggest modern forest. South of Kielder is another of the Commission's largest forests, Wark, which extends almost to Hadrian's Wall.

At Hexham there is a small park with some interesting trees, including an oak planted in 1882 to celebrate the founding at that time of what is now the Royal Forestry Society of England, Wales and Northern Ireland at that place.

The National Trust's property at Wallington, Cambo (near Morpeth) has interesting trees and woodland.

NOTTINGHAMSHIRE

This county will always be associated with Sherwood and the legendary Robin Hood. Today, the Sherwood Forest of the Forestry Commission covers woodlands not only in Nottinghamshire but spreading into Derbyshire and Yorkshire; there appear to be no forest walks within its confines. Just recently the County Council has made 86 acres near Edwinstowe, including the Major Oak, into a county park.

Much of the area within or adjoining the old forest is now covered by the Dukeries, the great estates of Clumber, Thoresby, Rufford and Welbeck. In and around them can still be found the relics of great oaks, often with legendary stories attached.

Clumber Park, south east of Worksop, is National Trust property. It includes the longest avenue in England. The trees are the European lime planted in 1840 in double rows for a length of three miles, plate 14.

Thoresby Hall, near Budby, open on stated occasions, has fine trees around it.

OXFORDSHIRE

Oxfordshire was a favourite royal hunting ground, being accessible to London. Wychwood, still an element in place names, was in the west (there are still considerable private woodlands around the river Evenlode which cuts through it); Shotover Forest reached almost to Oxford itself on the east. So did Woodstock, said to be the first forest to be placed within a wall, and when given to the victorious Marlborough it covered 2,119 acres. On the north east Bernwood spread over from Buckinghamshire. In the south east, possibly the Chiltern scarp was wooded. In the time of Elizabeth I, unlike much royal hunting country, it was well wooded. Subsequently the density of the woodland decreased.

Today, the Forestry Commission holds little forest land in Oxfordshire. Its Bernwood Forest still spreads over from Buckinghamshire, and some of its Chiltern forest spreads from that county and Hertfordshire.

The most interesting collections of trees are to be found in Oxford itself. The University Botanic Garden opened in 1621 as the Oxford Physic Gardens—the first of its kind in England—though not large, has fine old specimens of the same type of service tree as was found in Wyre Forest, Worcestershire (*Sorbus domestica*), the 'Japanese' pagoda tree (*Sophora japonica*), plate 25, the Kentucky coffee tree (*Gymnocladus dioicus*) and the rare persimmon (*Diospyros virginiana*) among others. In the riverside fields known as The Parks is a considerable variety of trees, some particularly interesting: there is available a *Guide to the Trees and Shrubs in the University Parks Oxford* (Oxford University Press).

The National Trust has two properties of beech woodland on the scarp of the Chilterns, Aston Wood, north west of Stokenchurch on the A40 road, and Watlington Park, a mile south east of that town.

The National Trust property of Buscot has a remarkable garden designed by Harold Peto early this century making extensive use of trees; there are subsequent large scale plantings of avenues and other features.

Open at stated times is Blenheim Palace, the park of which is 'Capability' Brown's greatest achievement. It contains superb trees. Also regularly open is Rousham House at Steeple Aston with one of the first gardens in the new eighteenth century landscape style designed by William Kent in which the woodland and magnificent specimen trees hang above the river Cherwell.

SALOP

The county ranges over the fertile Vale of Severn—predominantly agricultural—still scattered with magnificent oaks—to the outlying woods of Wyre on the south east, with remains of the pioneering areas of the iron industry around and eastwards of Wellington (which had devastating effects on the adjoining woodlands), then spreads westwards to the hilly Welsh border country (in this part the bird cherry, *Prunus padus,* a native tree with a restricted habitat, is often seen), and in the south west touches the wooded districts of Herefordshire.

Today, the most interesting and beautiful woodland area lies to the west of Ludlow spreading north west to Clun and roughly south west to Presteign, while southwards it spreads into Herefordshire around Shobdon. It embraces the woodland of much of the country described in Housman's *Shropshire Lad;* the rivers Teme, Lugg and Onny cut their ways between the hilly land often now regaining their lost tree cover.

The Forestry Commission has a major plantation in this area. Its Mortimer Forest, a new name in remembrance of the powerful medieval Marcher family, covers over 13 square miles, not in one block but scattered in perhaps twenty different holdings. The biggest, adjoining Ludlow, stretching south west, includes Bringewood Chase, whose trees were destroyed by the establishment in 1584 of Bringewood Forge on the river Teme (the name still remains on the Ordnance Map). South of this lies High Vinnals, said to have been the woodland in which Milton placed his *Comus,* the masque performed at Ludlow Castle nearby. A number of small roads wind among this remote and interesting district, with its occasional wide views both towards the Welsh Borders and over the Severn Vale in the Midlands.

The Royal Forestry Society's property nearby at Leighton is a remarkable piece of woodland which combines the Charles Ackers redwood grove with the Naylor pinetum. The main grove has thirty-three coast redwoods of California which are reputed to have been brought over and planted in 1858. Redwoods like these are among the tallest trees that grow in the British Isles. The pinetum is an exceptionally rich collection of over a hundred conifers, among which are Brewer's spruce, Chilean incense cedar, Irish juniper, Lebanon cedar (see plate 24), maidenhair tree and swamp cypress (see plate 26). All trees (vandals permitting) have their labels. R.F.S. leaflets are available from 102 High Street, Tring, Herts.

The National Trust's property at Attingham Park at Atcham 4 miles south east of Shrewsbury is a contrast to the romantic west of the county in its calm, park landscape created by Humphry Repton in 1797 around the little river Tern near where it joins the swelling Severn.

Open at stated times is the Earl of Bradford's Weston Park near Shifnal. Beside the house is an ornamental woodland walk around and beyond the lake containing many exceptionally fine trees. On a terrace in front of the house is possibly the largest oriental plane (*Platanus orientalis*) in England. The park is one of 'Capability' Brown's finest and largest, with three lakes, and whose magnificent trees are regularly replaced as they fall into decay.

Hodnet Hall near Market Drayton is also regularly open. The large garden around a string of lakes, made in the last few decades by the late Brigadier Heber Percy, contains many interesting trees.

SOMERSET

In early times Exmoor was the principal royal forest in the county, probably much the same as it is now—an expanse of bleak moorland edged by wooded coombs.

The Forestry Commission has a big forest in the Quantocks, and an excellent guide to the Quantock Forest Trail, just south of Nether Stowey, with excellent drawings making easy the identification of the principal species grown. The same applies to the guide to the Castle Neroche Forest Trail, about 5 miles south of Taunton.

The National Trust has some good woodlands on its properties. In the woods on its big Holnicate estate south of Porlock are some remarkable walnut trees—an unusual sight in woodland.

Many private gardens in the sheltered combes have interesting trees, but few seem to be regularly open to the public.

STAFFORDSHIRE

This county with the Black Country to the south and the Potteries in the north has had much of its woodland destroyed. The remains and records of the famous oaks at Bagots Park give an idea of what splendid trees once grew there.

The most widely visited woodland is undoubtedly Cannock Chase—once densely wooded. Then in 1550 the first Lord Paget had a licence for iron, using in the new blast furnace all timber trees of oak, ash and beech. Within thirty years these had mostly been consumed. The heath-like area, in which are coal mines and gravel pits, remained scrub until 1920 when the Forestry Commission began reafforesting most of its 6,000 acres predominantly with pines. Most of it now has public access; the natural history of the area is interesting and there is a deer museum. A number of important roads cut through it; the main body of the forest lies between Penkridge and Rugeley. There is a good guide published by the Forestry Commission (H.M.S.O.). Just to its north in the valley of the Trent lies the National Trust property of Shugborough Park with a fine eighteenth century landscape.

The once famous Needwood Forest, west of Burton-on-Trent, disafforested in 1802, is now little more than remembered by its place names, other than a Duchy of Lancaster forest, though in 1838 the district was still noted for its huge holly trees. In medieval times the lime was a common tree there. It has one honour as being, perhaps, the first forest to have a book published on its forest walks—and a poetic one at that. Although Thomas Gisborne, author of *Walks in a Forest* (1794) does not mention Needwood by name, he lived at Yoxall within it. He described the trees, forest history—human and natural—adding many moral reflections.

The most attractive woodland scenery is in the north east of the county. Hawksmoor, just north east of Cheadle, is an interesting, largely wooded area belonging to the National Trust. The enormous and dramatic garden of Alton Towers in the Churnet Valley some 5 miles eastward of Cheadle just off B5032, begun at the beginning of last century by an Earl of Shrewsbury and developed by his descendants, is planted with many fine specimens, as is Trentham Park on the southern borders of Stoke-on-Trent on A34; both these are open daily.

There is also a good collection of trees in the garden and park of Sandon Hall on A51 between Stone and Rugeley, opened on stated dates.

SUFFOLK

Though Suffolk is not a heavily wooded county (though becoming increasingly more so) it is one whose trees are of considerable interest. In the north west and including the adjoining Norfolk is the Breckland, the driest district of the British Isles and one where severe frosts are suffered in summer. It has a strange soil consisting of chalk overlaid by sand. In Suffolk this area reaches to Brandon, famous for its prehistoric flint mines, and Mildenhall where the equally famous Roman treasure was found. The recent developments in forestry, however, are centred on Thetford in Norfolk and are referred to under that county.

Otherwise Suffolk is a county of contrasts. There is heath-land, such as is found around Newmarket (just within the county on the west) and Martlesham to the east by the Deben estuary. The trees here are typical of all heathland; in some areas the roads and estates are bordered by old Scots pines acting as breaks against the bitter winds from the north sea. Set against this are the fertile vales seen so often in the pictures of Constable. Here grow elm trees, often variations of *Ulmus carpinifolia,* and other kinds with small leaves as well as the wych elm. They often dominate the roadside and, indeed, the landscape. The hedgerow elm of the midlands is absent. Their identification sets many problems.

Alders and willows abound in the damp and watery places, which provide excellent ground for the cricket-bat willow; the watermark disease to which it is subject in many localities seems less prevalent here. The small, bluish-leaved trees planted orchardwise are a feature of the landscape in the southern part of the county.

Just inland from the coast there are now considerable forests of conifers, the Corsican pine being common. They are particularly in evidence on the landward side between Aldeburgh and Dunwich: the Forestry Commission has its Aldewood Forest here.

A tree not uncommonly planted not far from the sea as avenues or to form windbreaks is the holm oak (*Quercus ilex*) which withstands the salty winds in temperatures much lower than those experienced in its natural habit.

A remarkable and perplexing district is the mixed and weird-looking woodland lying between the rivers Alde and Deben. Called Staverton Thicks, it consists of most ancient oaks—some no more than queer, clumsy shells—equally old hollies and rowans. There are many seedlings of holly and some of rowan. The place has an eerie silence; little seems known of its history.

SURREY
(see also Kent and Sussex)

Surprisingly, this now suburbanised county has one of the highest percentages of woodland in the country. It is geographically, along with Kent and Sussex, part of the Weald, well described by C. A. Barrington in *Forestry in the Weald*. (Forestry Commission Booklet No. 22). H.M.S.O.

It was in olden times a producer of hazel, grown under oak, for hurdles and still has much chestnut coppice. It is good pine country; it is said that Scots pines re-introduced from Scotland in the reign of James I quickly became naturalised and self-sown examples are typical on the heathy land. Forest-grown Corsican pine does exceedingly well. Birch is prolific on the lighter ground.

The Forestry Commission's holding is small. Alice Holt Forest, ancient woodland and one of the oldest state forests in the country, on the western boundary of the county, is important as including within its bounds the Commission's research headquarters.

In its Abinger Forest, there are three walks in the Ranmore area, 2 miles north-west of Dorking, each beginning from the National Trust car park on its Ranmore Common property.

Its greatest attraction to those interested in trees lies, however, in the great collections at the Royal Horticultural Society's Wisley Gardens and the later one at Winkworth Arboretum.

The Royal Horticultural Society's Gardens at Wisley, near Ripley, originated in an ancient piece of typical Surrey oak woodland, ancient and undisturbed, with deep soil rich in leaf mould. This was bought by G. F. Wilson in 1878 and here he made the first woodland garden, naturalizing plants from all parts of the temperate world. In 1903 it came into the charge of the Royal Horticultural Society, which has developed and extended it greatly in the subsequent years. Again, as at Kew, a great variety of trees is found growing in many places, while there is a considerable pinetum and very good collections of the so-called 'flowering' trees such as cherries and crab-apples. Wisley is open to the general public on week-days throughout the year; an excellent guide book is available.

An even more recent collection of trees is to be seen at the National Trust's Winkworth Arboretum three miles south east of Godalming. It was made by an enthusiastic arboriculturist, Dr. Wilfrid Fox, and given by him to the Trust in 1952. It is particularly rich in the trees of western and central China—maples, rowans and service trees introduced during the opening decades of this century. It is open free, daily throughout the year.

There are many exceptionally fine Surrey collections in private houses which are regularly opened at stated times—others, it seems, are not available to the public.

An excellent and delightful place of this type that is frequently open during the season is Grayswood Hill at Haslemere, situated with extensive views over Sussex. Planting was begun last century by the importation of seedlings, many from the Far East, and has been continued by subsequent owners. There are outstanding specimens, including *Pinus montezumae, Liquidambar styraciflua* and *Nothofagus* species.

Surrey is also interesting on account of its long established nursery trade. Many introductions from the eighteenth century onwards were first cultivated in the county.

SUSSEX
(see also Kent and Surrey)

This county probably still has a higher proportion of its surface under timber than any other—its near rivals being Surrey and Hampshire. In 1724 Defoe wrote that here 'the great foundaries, or iron-works carried on at such prodigious expense of wood, that even in a country* almost all over-run with timber, they begin to complain of the consuming it for those furnaces, and leaving the next age to want timber for their navies: I must own, however, that I found that complaint perfectly groundless, the three counties of Kent, Sussex and Hampshire, (all of which be contiguous to one another) being one inexhaustible store-house of timber never to be destroyed, but by a general conflagration, and able at this time to supply timber to rebuild all the royal navies in Europe.' That gives an idea of the richness of the woodlands, but it was not a true assessment. He also tells us that the great trees needed for the navy were getting further and further away from water—the best means of transport—and that near Lewes

* this is in the sense of countryside.

he saw trees so heavy that they could only be moved through the deep soil in dry summer hauled by twenty-two oxen, to Maidstone and thence by water to Chatham. If the summer was wet, the journey might taken even three years. We cannot accept Defoe's statement other than as to the appearance of the density of the wood, as just thirty years later it was his own son-in-law who pioneered the new, badly needed plantings of oak.

Geographically, Sussex belongs to the Weald—together with Surrey and Kent (which see). The area as a whole is described by C. A. Barrington in *Forestry in the Weald,* (Forestry Commission Booklet No. 22) published by H.M.S.O.; it has excellent illustrations.

There are Forestry Commission walks in the large Slindon Forest lying to the north of Chichester, the Selshurst Park walk near East Dean, the Northwood walk near Eartham and the Marden walk near Stoughton. In the Friston Forest north of Eastbourne there is Wilmington walk near West Dean, and in St. Leonards south of Horsham near Southwater there is another.

The big Queen Elizabeth Forest lies across the border of Sussex and Hampshire; there is a walk beginning near Buriton.

The most important National Trust woodland property is Wakehurst Place, near Ardingly. It has now been leased as an extension to the Royal Botanic Gardens, Kew. Here, 120 acres of gardens with many fine trees, including a pinetum with rare examples, and 400 acres of woodland—all in a magnificent setting—the possibilities of further expansion of our National Collections are already being seized.

The Trust's famous property at Sheffield Park is a magnificent garden in which is a great variety of trees and shrubs planted most successfully for effect. Mr. A. G. Soames began it in 1909, in a late eighteenth century landscape setting, making—as is now apparent—original and wonderful use of the great variety of trees that had become available. These are at their most brilliant in autumn, but there is something of interest to see among the trees at all seasons.

There are many extremely interesting specimens at another Trust property, Nymans gardens at Handcross, including the giant-leaved poplar, *Populus lasiocarpa,* the rare *Tetracentron sinense* held by some to be among the most beautiful of all trees, and *Rhus potaninii* with dazzling autumn foliage. There are also valuable specimens in a pinetum.

Of private gardens open at stated times, Borde Hill near Haywards Heath has an exceptional collection of trees, especially rich in the east Asiatic species collected by Wilson, Forrest and Kingdon Ward—often raised from their seed—in the first decades of the present century. There are also good examples of trees from the southern hemisphere such as *Nothofagus* species and conifers not usually grown. Leonardslee near Horsham is also of considerable interest.

WARWICKSHIRE AND WEST MIDLANDS

Through Shakespeare's plays, as well as today's place names, Warwickshire is particularly associated with the Forest of Arden. In fact, there never was a royal forest with such a name in that situation. The north of the area, including what is now often referred to as the Birmingham plateau, the high land including that town and stretching southward until the land drops down to the vale of Shakespeare's Avon, was in early times densely wooded, and that is what eventually became known as Arden. The name, it seems, is not connected with woodland, and may relate to high or steep land, and have the same origin as the Ardennes in France. The present 'Arden' district was indeed the southern part of the ancient woodland that covered the high land in Staffordshire above the Trent valley north of Birmingham and the still wooded Feckenham district to the south west in Worcestershire.

Agriculture, industry and urbanization of the Arden area have now so altered the landscape that Warwickshire is now among the most lightly wooded counties in England. Many fine trees, mostly oaks are, however, scattered over it, as are many delightful small woods and copses.

In the north east of the area and on the outskirts of Birmingham is the interesting Sutton Park, now a most important recreational area almost entirely surrounded by housing. Considerable parts of it have never been enclosed and planted and may well carry the descendants of the ancient trees on this wooded plateau. Here woodland containing oaks, both pedunculate and sessile, holly, birch, rowans and occasional service trees, seldom growing densely on the light, gravelly soil, may be examined. In the damper parts, besides alders and willows, (particularly *Salix fragilis,* presumably originally planted) the downy birch, *B. pubescens* can be found. The colonization of areas following destruction by fire with dense growths of the verrucose birch can be seen, and there is interesting thorn scrub.

In the planted areas pines and larch are the commonest kinds.

In Birmingham itself, good specimens of ornamental trees grow in Cannon Hill and Highbury parks. Together with some fine old examples of our native trees there is plenty of scope for studying a variety of trees within them.

The City Museum has, in the Pinto collection, a remarkable assemblage of wooden artifacts of every possible kind.

Charlecote, a National Trust property near Stratford upon Avon, besides its deer park land with some grand old trees, had a very fine old elm avenue which survived the destruction of the old seventeenth century formal garden when it was land-scaped by 'Capability' Brown, but not elm disease.

Ragley Hall, near Alcester, and Warwick Castle—where 'Capability' Brown did some of his earliest work—are both well worth visiting arboriculturally; they are privately owned and opened on stated occasions.

WILTSHIRE

Wiltshire today has much of its area covered with down-land and the great plateau of Salisbury Plain where the soil is thin and chalky. On this, beech, ash, yew and the occasional whitebeam grow. In the shallow valleys there is deeper soil which carried deeper rooting trees. In recent years a great deal of this type of land that was open and grazed has been ploughed; the trees that were on it have gone as the huge ploughed fields spread—perhaps a danger ecologically.

Savernake, crossed by many roads and with both camping and picnic sites, for centuries owned and managed by a Warden, now the present Marquess of Ailesbury, but leased by him to the Forestry Commission, is an ideal spot to study this type of forest, its history and present use. In A.D. 1200 west to east it was about 15 miles at its widest, from north to south, approximately 9 miles. It covered some 100 square miles of untouched country, remaining as it had done for centuries. There was little woodland—perhaps only seven areas—interspersed with land that was ideal for the preservation of all kinds of game.

In the reign of Queen Elizabeth I it is known that this woodland had deteriorated badly. The oldest trees were dying, seedlings that should have replaced them were eaten by deer. Some outlying parts were turned to agriculture. The place was largely neglected until the time of Charles, Lord Bruce, who began to plant in about 1720. At his death in 1747 he had planted very extensively. He was responsible for the famous beech avenues, now decaying from old age and being carefully and unostentatiously replaced by the Forestry Commission. Subsequently, the forest has been well maintained, and care taken in its planning. For example in the second half of the eighteenth century the deer were put into enclosures. The first commercial planting of spruce and larch, together with more oak, ash, beech and chestnut took place between 1894 and 1911. Throughout its later history, down to the present activities of the Forestry Commission, the amenity and visual aspects of this lovely forest have had careful consideration.

There is a marked Postern Hill walk from and around the picnic place.

There are many other places in the county where fine trees may be examined closely. The National Trust's property of Stourhead at Stourton in the extreme south west of the county is one. Here Henry Hoare during the middle years of the eighteenth century created one of the first great landscape gardens, forming in a bleak valley a wonderful scene with a lake surrounded by woodland, mostly beech and spruce. At the end of the century a walk was made round the lake and a collection of exotic trees begun which has continued to the present time: many of the specimens now reach record-breaking size.

Private estates with fine trees open at stated times include Wilton House just outside Salisbury where probably the first Lebanon cedars in this country were planted about 1638. Their offspring are now towering specimens on the lawn. There are also particularly fine trees at Longleat House, near Warminster and Corsham Court near Chippenham.

YORKSHIRE

Yorkshire, by far the largest county in England, has great variation in types of land and a consequent variety in its trees and forestry. Its long coastline on the east, owing to the presence of the North Sea, results in an area subject to cold winters with warm summers and a low rainfall while on the west of the county it approaches the wetter climate of the north-western districts. Centred on, say, Harrogate, one is within reach of great variations in types of forestry and a fine variety of trees. Woodland in private hands covers about twice the area of that held by the Commission; a feature of this is that much of the county's magnificent mature sycamore lies in the older, usually inherited woods (this includes trees with the highly valued 'curly' grain used for decorative plywood).

There were royal forests of considerable importance in Norman times. Galtres, adjoining the gates of York was one, Pickering (now once again celebrated for its woods) was another, famed for its boars. Deer were abundant. Wolves were still present near Richmond in 1369.

As has been mentioned earlier, the first great assault upon

our woodlands in the wilder places came with the ranching of sheep by the Cistercians at Rievaulx Abbey north west of Helmsley; they later had Byland, Fountains and Jervaulx within the county. The Yorkshire wool trade, inimical to trees, became of great importance. Yorkshire's industrial prosperity later led to the development of the great private estates, already mentioned.

The Commission has made a feature of nature trails in its *Pickering District Forest Map,* a most useful publication. This covers an area lying within 4 miles of Scarborough and stretching some 16 miles westward and a similar distance north and south. Separate leaflets cover the Silpho trail and forest walk to Allerston, the Wykeham forest trail, the Sneverdale trail and the Newton Dale trail.

There is also a useful *Bishop Wood Forest Guide* to this forest which lies 12 miles south of York, between Sherburn-in-Elmet and Selby.

There is much else to be seen in the county.

The magnificent ruin of Fountains Abbey is a relic of the Cistercians. It is a typical Cistercian site in the deep valley of the small river Skell. The trees—mostly oak and wych elm—are enormous. Walking down the river, the path goes between huge sombre yews and enters the old formal garden of Studley Royal, the house no longer existing. Here again there are superb trees. From it, Studley Royal park is entered and Ripon, 3 miles away can be reached. In the park were some of the biggest and oldest oaks in England but many were thrown in the 1962 gale. The estate now belongs to the county council and is open daily.

In contrast are the modern Harlow Car Gardens, the 'northern Wisley'. Situated on part of the site of the ancient forest of Knaresborough, and begun in 1948 they already contain a very interesting collection of ornamental trees. The gardens are about a mile and a half from the centre of Harrogate on the Otley Road.

Of the houses open to the public at stated times, Rudding Park, three miles to the south east of Harrogate has interesting trees in the gardens and is set in a fine Repton landscape. Ripley Castle, 4 miles north of Harrogate has good trees in and around the garden. Leeds is exceptional in its public parks, their woodlands and remarkable trees, though smoke pollution does not suit conifers. The Hollies and adjoining estates at Headingley, with woodlands, streams and ravines, give many surprises by the trees found there, well underplanted with shrubs. There are good trees, too, in the famous Roundhay Park, while in the Temple Newsam grounds, a fine 'Capability' Brown landscape is being rehabilitated. These are open daily.

Near Leeds, 8 miles north on the Harrogate road, is Harewood House with one of the most famous of 'Capability' Brown's landscapes, though damage (now being repaired) was done to some of the fine trees by the 1962 gale. It is opened on stated dates, as is Castle Howard, north east of York and west of Malton, with fine avenues and stately trees in the wonderfully landscaped park.

The modern gardens of Newby Hall south east of Ripon in a Victorian setting, also have a good selection of trees.

GLOSSARY

Arboretum (plural arboreta): a collection of all kinds of living trees.

Arboriculture: now usually considered to be the cultivation of trees of all kinds for ornamental purposes—different from silviculture (q.v.).

Bole: the part of a tree trunk below the first main branch.

Broad-leaved: dicotyledonous trees as distinct from conifers; also called hardwoods—neither terms are always literally accurate.

Cleave: to split timber longitudinally with an axe.

Conifer: trees whose fruit is a cone in between whose scales the seed is loosely held; the wood contains resin canals not present in hardwoods.

Coppice: a tree which is cut to ground level at regular intervals causing it to send up a number of shoots (coppice shoots or poles) used for various purposes.

Copse: originally a coppiced wood, but now applied to any small wood.

Cultivar: abnormal variants of plants cultivated by man which he maintains by special means of propagation e.g. the weeping ash whose seeds produce trees of the normal type and which, therefore, must be propagated by means such as grafting.

Deciduous: of a tree, one that drops all its leaves annually.

Evergreen: of a tree, one on which the individual leaves last for more than one year; they do, however, fall eventually—in most cases after three or four years. The result is that the tree is never leafless.

Exotic: introduced from overseas—the opposite to native (q.v.).

Fastigiate: a tree with branches that grow erect and largely parallel to one another e.g. Lombardy poplar.

Fir: now usually applied to the genera *Abies* (silver firs from the prominent silvery markings on the undersides of the leaves), *Picea* (spruce fir) and *Pseutotsuga,* Douglas firs, but from early times used in the vernacular for many conifers, particularly in Britain applied to the Scots pine.

Forest: formerly applied to areas under the royal forest laws, savagely directed towards preservation for hunting and not necessarily densely wooded. Except when the name lingers on from early times, now used, particularly by the Forestry Commission, for large areas of woodland managed principally for economic purposes.

Genus: the lowest main category of plant classification (plural, genera) and composed of species—e.g. *Abies, Acer,* etc. the names being either Latin or Latinised and often of ancient, sometimes unknown, origin or frequently modern —usually of honorific and even inconsequential—origin.

Hardwood: the same as broad-leaved (q.v.) and like that term, not always literally accurate e.g. the timber of poplars is physically quite soft.

Heart-wood: the hard, matured wood in the centre of a trunk, no longer growing, providing the strongest timber.

Hybrid: a cross between two kinds, usually due to the pollen of one being placed by man or naturally on the stigma of another, the resulting seedling partaking in certain qualities from both.

Introduced: the same as exotic (q.v.).

Maiden: a tree grown on single stem neither pollarded nor coppiced.

Native: a plant growing in Britain naturally since before our island was separated from the continent of Europe and not introduced by man.

Naturalised: an exotic plant that seeds itself and produces succeeding generations without the direct aid of man, e.g. horse-chestnut, sycamore, or a native plant that spreads and so grows beyond its restricted natural territory e.g. Scots pine originally restricted to Scotland but naturalised for example in Surrey.

Pinetum (plural pineta): a collection of trees restricted to conifers—not necessarily pines.

Pollard: a tree regularly cut back at a height beyond the reach of grazing stock in the same manner as coppice (q.v.)

Regeneration, natural: a bit of forester's jargon meaning natural reproduction, i.e. trees that arise from self-sown seeds without the interference of man.

Sapwood: the wood of a tree between the bark and the heart-wood which is not yet mature and hardened.

Silviculture: now generally held to mean the cultivation of trees for timber as opposed to arboriculture (q.v.)

Softwood: a general term applied (often inaccurately) to conifers, as distinct from hardwood (q.v.)

Species: the fundamental unit in the botanical classification of plants, i.e. the different members within a genus. Specific names are Latinised and are generally descriptive, honorific or of obscure meaning. e.g. *Chamaecyparis lawsoniana,* the chamaecyparis named in honour of Lawson who introduced it; *Taxus baccata,* the yew bearing berries.

Variety: a minor variation within a species that breeds true.

FOR READING

The valuable series of *Booklets* and *Guides* to Forestry Commission properties are published by Her Majesty's Stationery Office (abbreviated to H.M.S.O. in the text) and are obtainable through booksellers and from the Stationery Office itself

The following books will be helpful:

Barber, P. and Lucas Phillips, C. E. *The Trees Around Us.* Weidenfeld & Nicolson (published in collaboration with the Royal Horticultural Society).

Edlin, H. L. *Wayside and Woodland Trees.* Warne.

Hadfield, M. *British Trees: a Guide for Everyman* (with a bibliography). Dent.

Hadfield, M. *Landscape with Trees* (an historical account). Country Life.

Hadfield, M. *Your Book of Trees* (for younger readers). Faber.

Hyde, H. A. *Welsh Timber Trees* (equally applicable to England). National Museum of Wales.

Laidlaw, W. B. R. *Guide to British Hardwoods.* Hill.

Mitchell, A. *Field Guide to the Trees of Britain and Northern Europe.* Collins.

Nicholson, B. E. and Clapham, A. R. *The Oxford Book of Trees.* Oxford University Press.

INDEX

94

INDEX